# Your GPS to Employment Success

# Your GPS to Employment Success

## How to Find and Succeed in the Right Job

Beverly A. Williams

BUSINESS EXPERT PRESS

*Leader in applied, concise business books*

*Your GPS to Employment Success: How to Find and Succeed in the Right Job*

Copyright © Business Expert Press, LLC, 2021.

Cover design by Charlene Kronstedt

Illustrations by Aaron Wms; Cartoon Artwork by Lyman Dally

Interior design by Exeter Premedia Services Private Ltd., Chennai, India

First published in 2021 by
Business Expert Press, LLC
222 East 46th Street, New York, NY 10017
www.businessexpertpress.com

ISBN-13: 978-1-95334-996-5 (paperback)
ISBN-13: 978-1-95334-997-2 (e-book)

Business Expert Press Business Career Development Collection

Collection ISSN: 2642-2123 (print)
Collection ISSN: 2642-2131 (electronic)

First edition: 2021

10 9 8 7 6 5 4 3 2 1

# Dedication

To anyone who has been told or made to feel they are not enough or cannot be successful or otherwise feel marginalized:

*Believe you can and you're halfway there.*

Theodore Roosevelt,
26th president of the United States

# Description

Economies had barely recovered from the Great Recession of 2008 when the COVID-19 pandemic moved swiftly around the world threatening to devastate global economies and their populations yet again. Inevitably, unemployment followed. Anyone looking for employment or a promotion in a mercurial economic environment can find useful tips and information in *Your GPS to Employment Success: How to Find and Succeed in the Right Job*.

This book is a career resource that contains a treasure trove of straightforward, pithy job search and career advice, 125 tips, and stories from an employment expert. It is a career advancement and networking guide that also identifies inconvenient truths that are not commonly known but are helpful to have in your career toolkit.

*Your GPS to Employment Success* also addresses

- The importance of preparing mentally, physically, and emotionally for a roller-coaster job search.
- How to adopt NBA star forward LeBron James's career strategy for personal career goals.
- How to develop a career plan and strategy, and the need to execute a career strategy.
- How to look for employment in a virtual world.
- How a former NFL athlete asked a stranger for help and changed the trajectory of his life.

The author also provides a career toolkit that contains informative, time-saving material.

## Keywords

internship; intern; career resources; career guide; career advice; career planning; career advancement; career counseling; career change; career coaching; job search; your employment; employment; networking

# Contents

# Testimonials

*"Your GPS to Employment Success takes readers through the various scenarios they are likely to encounter in their job search and career advancement. By using well-placed examples and bullet points for additional focus, this book has a feeling that readers are being mentored."* —**Michelle Lopez, Former SVP, Chief Employment Counsel, MTV Networks/Viacom CBS**

*"Your GPS to Employment Success: How to Find and Succeed in the Right Job, is a comprehensive guide that provides practical, realistic and current advice on how to find a job, navigate the internet, network, interview and be successful in today's business world. Beverly Williams provides tools and templates to aid the job seeker and delivers the material in an easy to read instructional format."* —**Thomas Duym, Former Vice President—Risk Management, Automatic Data Processing - ADP**

# Foreword

Beverly Williams is the ultimate no-nonsense adviser. She doesn't bother telling you what would be comforting to hear—in a highly competitive job market, you don't need that. Beverly tells you what you need to know.

*Your GPS to Employment Success* contains 125 specific tips to help you navigate today's ever more challenging employment environment. Along the way, it includes inspirational quotations, success stories, and cautionary tales. On topics ranging from making a good impression on a prospective employer to averting social media pitfalls, the book provides guidance that is insightful and easy to absorb.

It has never been more important for job seekers and job holders to maximize opportunities and avoid costly errors. *Your GPS to Employment Success* is your guide to mastering today's work-related challenges.

Brad R. Roth
Professor of Political Science & Law
Wayne State University
Detroit, MI

# Acknowledgments

Valeria Jacobs Andrews

Mary Flamer

Katie Gooler

Wade J. Henderson

Jessica Ken Kwofie

Ellen Nelson

Illene Ocampo

Dansby White

Thank you for your time, suggestions, and support.

# General Information

This book is provided as a practical guide and resource for general information on employment-related issues. While the author, editor, and publisher have made efforts to assure the accuracy of the material in this book as of August 1, 2020, it should not be treated as a basis for formulating business and legal decisions without individualized legal and professional advice. In legal matters, no publication can take the place of professional advice given with full knowledge of the specific circumstances of each matter and the actual practices of the employer.

This book contains links to third-party websites ("External Sites"). These links are provided solely as a convenience to you and not as an endorsement by us of the content on such External Sites. The content of such External Sites is developed and provided by others. You should contact the site administrator or webmaster for those External Sites if you have any concerns regarding such links or any content located on such External Sites.

We are not responsible for the content of any linked External Sites and do not make any representations regarding the content or accuracy of materials on such External Sites. You should take precautions when downloading files from all websites to protect your computer from viruses and other destructive programs. If you decide to access linked External Sites, you do so at your own risk.

The author, editor, and publisher make no representation or warranty, express or implied, as to the completeness, correctness, or utility of the information contained in this book and assume no liability of any kind whatsoever resulting from the use or reliance upon its contents. The references and advice are provided based on professional experiences and observations, and should be considered along with the reader's individual circumstances.

# Introduction

**Your GPS to Employment Success:** *How to Find and Succeed in the Right Job* provides career advice as dos and don'ts, tips, stories, and cautionary tales. The material and content provided in this book are not a substitute for existing career counseling programs, materials, and human capital. Instead, it is intended to supplement what is currently in place, and in the future.

There is a wealth of free information on the Internet. Unfortunately, most people do not know what to look for and how to use it optimally. *Your GPS to Employment Success* is a resource that strives to enhance job seekers' employment journey.

Be mindful, however, that there simply is no substitute for, among other things, persistence, old-school and new-school networking, attention to detail, a positive attitude, reasonable expectations, and hard work. Set career goals; develop a career plan; and execute the plan.

*For success, attitude is equally as important as ability.*
—Walter Scott, Scottish novelist

# CHAPTER 1

# Prepare...Plan...Persist... Persevere

*Many employees realize they will need to switch careers at some stage in their life. Not only has the job-for-life disappeared, but the career-for-life is going the same way.*

—Mike Webster, Kelly Services Executive
Vice President and General Manager

## Reflections

How you approach your employment journey is crucial. Each day, prepare yourself mentally, emotionally, and physically. Develop a strategic plan and execute it. Persist with your efforts in furtherance of your goals and objectives. Persevere through negative responses, if any, and the absence of responses.

## Prepare

**TIP 1-1 View and prepare for your job search through a lens that presumes the worst job market ever regardless of the state of the economy and your prospects.**

Solely for the purpose of gauging the effort required to achieve the goal of your job search, ignore the ebb and flow of global and national economies and their effect on job availability. Prepare to compete for employment opportunities in the worst possible job market.

If you approach your journey through that lens, you will be prepared to compete for employment regardless of the state of the economy and the job market.

**TIP 1-2 List what you want to accomplish each day.**

The evening before you begin your job search, make a list of tasks to be completed the following day. Set the clock, rise at the same time each day, work out, and eat breakfast. These daily tasks can be checked off as completed at the end of each day. Decide how you will journal your experience, either on the computer, in a notebook, or whatever facilitates your thinking.

Your list should include reading the morning news and job boards, conducting research about businesses and people associated with those businesses, drafting resumes and cover letters, and networking via e-mail and social media. In addition, prepare a list of personal consultants who can contribute to your job search with informed guidance. Including these people on your daily schedule for coffee, for example, can provide a healthy sounding board for your progress and keep you focused. Such personal consultants should be well-informed friends, family members, and spiritual and political leaders.

Preparation may increase your ability to cope with the trials and tribulations that accompany the negative and positive aspects of employment pursuits. Establishing a routine and committing your daily schedule to writing will help you remain focused. If necessary, conspicuously post the list of tasks and your schedule so it is easy to follow. Nothing must fall through the cracks.

**TIP 1-3   Use music to motivate and inspire you and change your mood.**

Listening to music may not only be good for your health,[1] it may ease your transition through the ups and downs of your job search. Create playlists that include upbeat music with or without lyrics or both versions.

---

[1] Heid, M. 2018. "You Asked: Is Listening to Music Good For Your Health?" TIME, April 26, 2018, https://time.com/5254381/listening-to-musichealth-benefits/; Edwards Van, V. 2019. "The Benefits of Music: How the Science of Music Can Help You." *Science of People,* https://scienceofpeople. com/ benefits-music/ FnH "Can Listening to Music Bring Actual Health Benefits?" June 26, 2019, https://foodnhealth.org/can-listening-to-musicbring-actual-health-benefits/

Get started with the *Gonna Fly Now* (Theme from Rocky)[2] and *Roar*[3] by Katy Perry.

*The Climb*[4] by Miley Cyrus is calmer, and perhaps may ease you into the conclusion of your day. Add personal favorites and play them randomly to add an element of surprise to your musical experience.

### TIP 1-4 Train like an olympian. (Consult a physician before you begin any fitness program.)

Achieving an Olympic medal undeniably requires single-minded focus and unwavering commitment. Visualize Olympic medalists who train relentlessly. To be successful, they train to condition themselves to compete in rigorous Olympic events.

Although there is no guarantee that their hard work will yield Olympic medals, they nonetheless put in the time and effort. Even the possibility that they will win a medal is worth the sacrifices they make. You are developing rigor for your job search.

You may find that you have more energy at the end of the day if you begin it with physical activity. Outdoor activities, such as cycling, walking, jogging, or swimming are free. If you can afford a gym you can have not only the benefit of physical activity but networking opportunities as well. Listening to upbeat music while you exercise may also leave you in an upbeat mood when you finish.

Never let inclement weather sidetrack your fitness efforts. Search the Internet and social media platforms for free streaming and online, in-home exercise videos. Join a neighborhood community center, check out videos from the library, utilize exercise videos on cable or purchase them.

In addition to exercise, balanced meals and healthy eating also keep minds sharp and bodies healthy. Given the limited time and energy available in a 24-hour day, focus and staying on task are necessary.

---

[2] Conti, B. 1976. "Composer; Capitol Records." https://soundtrack.net/album/rocky-capitol/

[3] Perry, K., J.M. Martin, Dr. M.M. Luke, and S.T. Hudson. 2013. "Capitol Records." Released August 10, 2013, https://lyrics.com/lyric/30485320/Katy+Perry/Roar

[4] Alexander, J., and J. Mabe. 2009. Writers, from *Hannah Montana: The Movie*. Walt Disney, https://songfacts.com/facts/miley-cyrus/the-climb

You will likely get from your employment search and efforts to gain a promotion what you put into them. Consistent effort, follow-up, networking, job-board searches, and résumé revisions are a few of the tasks critical for employment success.

Olympian Brendon Rodney agrees that people who are looking for employment should establish a daily routine by:

1. Getting plenty of rest
2. Eating healthy
3. Exercising
4. Planning and organizing daily tasks
5. Remaining focused on completing those tasks and achieving your goals
6. Taking a break periodically to enjoy yourself, and then beginning again

According to Brendon, rest and periodic breaks are important. Brace yourself for the drain on your energy.[5]

**TIP 1-5 Stay in shape or get into shape for your health and to enhance your personal appearance.**
Weight is a sensitive subject but one that should be addressed. Personal struggles aside, you do not have to be a lean, mean employment-seeking machine. You should know, however, that being overweight may affect your employment success.

It is no secret that being overweight contributes to medical issues. It is also common knowledge that health care premiums (a portion of which may be paid by employers) are expensive. There is no sign that premium costs are going to get cheaper.

If you do not have health issues and you are satisfied with how you look, do not change unless you want to do so. There is more acceptance of diversity in body type, ethnicity, and hairstyles now than in the past.

Be mindful, however, that physical appearance is more important in some industries than in others. Fashion and retail, client-facing sales, and on-air media roles are just a few industries and positions where appearance is client, customer, and viewer driven.

---

[5] *Telephone Interview with Olympic Medalist, Brendon Rodney* in August 2020.

If you decide to trim down, find a workout partner to join you in your fitness routine. It is easier to maintain a program if there is someone to keep you company while you exercise.

Make sure your partner is reliable and committed to achieving results. You could also create a networking opportunity through the people you meet on the track or at the gym.

### TIP 1-6 Manage your mindset.

Managing the stressors of life, including the stress that accompanies seeking employment, is not easy. Whatever your employment situation, your mental and physical well-being are critical to your success in finding a job and as an employee. Daily meditation can relieve stress and anxiety by clearing your head and placing you in a state of mind that permits you to concentrate on your job search or efforts to earn a promotion.

Take advantage of online resources, group chats, and networking opportunities.[6] Explore available online meditation tools and recordings to find one suitable for you. Mindfulness, "the basic human ability to be fully present, aware of where we are and what we're doing, and not overly reactive or overwhelmed by what's going on around us,"[7] may benefit you.

Focus on self-care.[8] Find videos that offer yoga or guided meditation. You can start with a 10-minute video and increase the time gradually. The goal is to be healthy and ready when opportunity knocks.

Do not be embarrassed if you become overwhelmed or feel *blue*. Acknowledge how you feel by telling someone such as your medical practitioner or clergy.

Do not struggle alone. Tell someone who will help you get either professional or family support.

---

[6] Tabone, Maria, B.A., M.A., and M.S. 2020. "Your Employment Matters with Beverly Williams Podcast." *Stress Management During a Pandemic,* https://youremploymentmatters.com/

[7] The Mindful Staff. 2014. "Mindful Blog." *What is Mindfulness?* October 6, 2014, https://mindful.org/what-is-mindfulness/

[8] Tabone, *Stress Management During a Pandemic.*

**TIP 1-7 Manage your expectations.**

**TIP 1-8 Make sure your expectations are reasonable and realistic.**

The pursuit of employment and on-the-job success, especially in competitive job markets, requires managing mental, physical, and emotional health. Thus, it is important to manage expectations. Do not expect all resumes to be acknowledged or to receive responses to all e-mails, texts, and telephone calls.

Depending on your personal circumstances, financial problems may worsen. How you manage these challenges is wholly within your control.

Your job search should be directed toward a job that you are qualified for. You should be able to articulate persuasively the value you bring, and why you should be hired. If you do not overreach for a position the emotional ups and downs of your employment journey should be more manageable.

If, however, you apply for jobs that you are not qualified for and you approach your job search cavalierly, save your time. You probably will not be hired unless you have a connection to someone to whom a huge favor is owed.

Generally, returning a favor is not an adequate incentive to hire an unqualified candidate. Depending on the caliber of qualified applicants, a favorable result for you may be simply moving to the next level of interviews. This will give you another opportunity. Make the best of it.

**TIP 1-9 Begin from a position of gratitude.**

Recognize that no one is obligated to help you get a job. Accordingly, be grateful for any assistance you receive. It may be a contact, an introductory meeting, or advice.

Whether you follow the advice or reach out to the contact or try to schedule the meeting, be grateful and gracious to the person who makes the offer. Acknowledge the generosity and express your gratitude to everyone including the custodian, doorman, administrative assistant, and anyone else, as appropriate.

## Plan

*One of the great liabilities of history is that all too many people fail to remain awake through great periods of social change. Every society has its protectors of status quo and its fraternities of the indifferent who are notorious for sleeping through revolutions. Today, our very survival depends on our ability to stay awake, to adjust to new ideas, to remain vigilant and to face the challenge of change.*

—Martin Luther King, Jr., minister, social activist,

and civil rights leader

### TIP 1-10 Embrace the new employment reality.

The mutual loyalty and trust that employers and their employees shared are no longer commonplace. As far too many employees have learned, loyalty and trust, while important, are not always reciprocal.

Jobs have been eliminated or moved elsewhere because of business decisions that favored outsourcing, restructuring, and maximizing profitability. Employment opportunities also have disappeared because of the impact of COVID-19.

More employees are working from home. Economist Susan Athey posits of telecommuting that, "[p]eople will change their habits, and some of these habits will stick. There's a lot of things where people are just slowly shifting, and this will accelerate that." [9]

The shrinking workplace physical footprint is indicative of a permanent shift toward telecommuting. Skills needed in this environment include (1) being organized, (2) technical prowess, (3) collaboration, (4) communication, and (5) self-motivation. [10]

For example, in order to maintain an air of professionalism, on-air media personalities and entertainers who do not have their support system have to learn how to apply makeup and manage their hair for a camera-ready appearance. Remote meetings with bosses should be handled as they would in the office. Not only should you be prepared but you should deliver your contribution clearly and succinctly.

---

[9] Guyot., K., and I.V. Sawhill. 2020. "Brookings' Blog." *Telecommuting will Likely Continue Long After the Pandemic,* April 6, 2020, https://brookings.edu/blog/upfront/2020/04/06/telecommuting-will-likely-continue-long-after-thepandemic/

[10] Vozza, S. 2020. "Fast Company' Blog." *5 Skills You Need to Demonstrate to Land a Remote Job,* April 17, 2020, https://fastcompany.com/90490491/5-skillsyou-need-to-demonstrate-to-land-a-remote-job

Working remotely does not appeal to everyone.[11] Be mindful, however, that technological developments drive business changes. They also affect the type of jobs and workers needed to perform those jobs.

There is no need to panic; the situation is not as bad as it may sound. Remember the Industrial Revolution? Gradually, but successfully, the world transitioned from an agrarian to an industrial society to an information technology juggernaut.

In stark contrast, a dozen years after the Great Recession of 2008, as the need to transition arose again, people seem to have failed to reconsider how to handle their employment matters. Rather than keeping abreast of industry developments, aggressively managing their careers, and proactively creating multiple income streams, it appears that the preexisting work routine resumed, albeit perhaps with different jobs and different employers.

Begin to think about your vision for your employment journey by considering whether you have a career strategy and a personal brand. It is never too early to visualize what you want to achieve. Realize that what you envision may change because of factors beyond your control.

## A Career Strategy Model

Thanks to LeBron James, the New Employment Reality arrived at the National Basketball Association (NBA) and is exemplified by his departure from the Cleveland Cavaliers for the Miami Heat in July 2010. Furthermore, this example represents a template for how to manage a career. Here are the steps in the template that LeBron James's move represents:

LeBron

1. Set realistic goals
2. Performed at the highest level
3. Allowed a reasonable time within which to achieve his goals
4. Objectively evaluated his talents and marketability
5. Relocated to another state to pursue and achieve his career goals

---

[11] Saunders, E.G. 2020. "Fast Company' Blog." *Panicked About Working from Home? Here's How to do it Right,* March 17, 2020, https://fastcompany. com/90477913/panicked-about-working-from-home-heres-how-to-do-it-right

LeBron James made a fortune playing with the Cleveland Cavaliers, but he had realistic, achievable career goals. He not only wanted to be on a championship team but also wanted to win NBA championships for multiple years.

After seven seasons with Cleveland, without bringing Cleveland an NBA championship, LeBron James decided to play for Miami for less money. LeBron felt that moving to Miami would give him the best opportunity to achieve his career goals. He was right.

With back-to-back successes, the Miami Heat was the NBA's 2012 and 2013 Championship Team. Career goals one and two ... ☑ and ☑! LeBron James left Miami and returned to Cleveland in 2014.

In 2016, leading the Cleveland Cavaliers, LeBron James won his third NBA Championship. In 2018, he bid farewell to Cleveland again. This time he joined the Los Angeles Lakers.

Two years later in October 2020, during the COVID-19 pandemic, LeBron James won a fourth NBA Championship against the Miami Heat, one of his former teams. Unquestionably, an admirable achievement that took, among other things, tremendous talent, focus, commitment, and teamwork.

**Do not get it twisted:** Make no mistake, LeBron James's approach will not work for everyone. We all know that he was, and amazingly still is, extremely talented and marketable.

Do not delude yourself, however, about your talents and marketability. An objective assessment of your skills and talents and on-the-job performance is critical.

### TIP 1-11 Do not overestimate your value on the open market.

The average person is not as talented as LeBron James, not as marketable, and probably employed or looking for employment in a workplace more mundane than the NBA. LeBron James nonetheless can be used to illustrate what it means to set career goals, manage a career, and create multiple income streams as he has in endorsements and entertainment projects.

Ask yourself objectively and honestly, am I in the position to create a New Employment Reality for myself? Remember, you must eat, pay rent, perhaps pay student loans, and fulfill other responsibilities.

Compare LeBron James's approach to his career with how Eve, an experienced, mature HR professional, handled her job search.

*Several years ago, Eve resigned as Director of Human Resources of a prominent teaching hospital. After two years, Eve decided that she missed the interaction with people, and wanted to return to work.*

*It was no surprise that Eve was called in for interviews by most of the companies that she applied to because her resume was impressive, and she had the desired pedigree. Her educational background included undergraduate and graduate degrees, and she had extensive industry work experience.*

*When Eve arrived for a series of interviews at a large health care organization, based on her polished appearance and professional demeanor, the staffing coordinator concluded that Eve could be the total package. The staffing coordinator was correct. Eve was an intelligent, articulate, and knowledgeable HR professional.*

*After her last interview, the hiring manager told Eve they were close to a decision among the top three applicants, one of whom was Eve. Inexplicably, Eve felt compelled to inform him quite candidly and unequivocally that she only wanted to work four days a week, and that she wanted Fridays off. In her opinion, any job could be performed in four days.*

*The hiring manager told Eve that she would hear from the staffing coordinator. Guess what? Eve is still waiting for the telephone call that will never come.*

Unlike LeBron James, Eve overestimated her value on the open market. Another difference between them is that LeBron was in the position to create a New Employment Reality for himself while Eve could only react to the New Employment Reality that had already been created.

Eve should have known that, given her profession and experience, there are many talented, unemployed professionals looking for jobs, and that no one (especially an HR professional) is irreplaceable.

Admittedly, people of all ages overplay their hands. Please do not be one of them.

**TIP 1-12 Identify or create your personal brand and protect it.**
Personal branding is a concept that more and more people recognize as an essential element in marketing themselves and managing their careers. Your personal brand is how people think of you and describe you. In some ways, it is outside your control, but you obviously have some influence over it.

Typically, employers look for hard skills or competencies and soft skills such as personal interactions. Examples of personal brand traits include verbal and written communication skills, personal appearance, technical proficiency, social media usage, and digital footprint.

**TIP 1-13 Dress, speak, and conduct yourself as you choose, but be prepared to accept the consequences.**

Your personal appearance and behavior on and off the job can impact whether you get hired and whether your career has an upward trajectory after you are hired. The way you think things should be, may not be the way things are. Often, the only reason for the difference is the business culture or a supervisor's idiosyncrasy.

For example, suppose the company you work for allows facial hair on men and open-toe[12] shoes for women, but your manager is an "old-school," 40-year-old who makes it clear that she thinks beards, moustaches, and peep-toe pumps are inconsistent with the conservative business image your employer wants to project.

As a job applicant or a new employee, you might have to make decisions about whether to exercise your right to assert your individuality. Are you willing to wear less flamboyant clothing and not have unusual hair colors and hairstyles? Are you willing to keep your opinions about politics, religion, and other potentially controversial subjects to yourself?

Seriously, there are conservative, less progressive companies that favor a more restrained style and their managers support the company's point of view. What do you do? Do you exercise your right, wear what you want, and possibly annoy your boss when you do, or do you conform? Fortunately, you have a choice, but you also have a decision to make.

**TIP 1-14 Think globally and nationally.**

Consider whether you are willing to relocate to another state or country to find employment. Your research may indicate that there is a dearth of jobs where you live or in nearby locations within commuting distance, and that is not likely to change in the future.

---

[12] Killinger. S. 2020. QVC Host. "Some Employers do not Want to See Your Toes No Matter How Pretty They Are." *QVC,* June 30, 2020.

Relocating to another state or country is an option. To make this option more palatable to you and your loved ones, focus on locations where family members or friends live.

### TIP 1-15 If you have a disability,[13] decide when or whether to disclose it.

Employment applications seek information about whether applicants have disabilities and whether they need a reasonable accommodation that will enable them to perform their jobs. If you are a person with a disability, who meets the qualifications of the position for which you applied, you will need to decide when or whether to disclose your disability to a prospective employer. The dilemma is whether to disclose a disability that is not discernible during an interview before you are offered a job.

The dilemma exists for several reasons. For example, a disabled person may not need a reasonable accommodation (as the law allows) every day because his or her disability (such as a medical condition) may be in remission. Many times, when people feel better, they believe their condition is no longer active. Unfortunately, they may be wrong.

### Persist

### TIP 1-16 Motivate yourself.

*Imagination is the beginning of creation. You imagine what you desire, you will what you imagine, and at last you create what you will.*
—George Bernard Shaw, Irish playwright and cofounder
of the London School of Economics

If a specific job is what your dreams are made of, or you see it as a means to acquire the things you want to do or purchase, find a picture that captures your vision of your ideal job. Take a picture of a vacation resort you want to visit; the motorcycle, car, or home you want to buy; or some other item that you dream of owning one day.

---

[13] Americans With Disabilities Act of 1990. Public Law 101-336. 108th Congress, 2nd session (July 26, 1990). https://dol.gov/general/topic/disability/ada

Next, place the picture in a beautiful frame pleasing to your eye, and tape unframed copies on your mirrors and on your refrigerator. If you are employed, place the framed picture on your desk at work; if you are unemployed, place it next to your bed so it is the last image you see before you go to sleep. Every time you get upset about your job or discouraged because you have been unable to find work, look at the picture and try harder...be persistent!

Tell yourself, "I can achieve anything that I put my mind and my best efforts toward achieving." After you tell yourself that you can do anything, and you set out to achieve your goal, do not let anyone tell you that you cannot or should not.

Keep in mind that success means different things to different people. Define career success on your terms according to your definition. If you have graduated from college and now you want to be a plumber, learn from experienced plumbers to be the best plumber you can be. If you want to be an executive, research what other successful executives have done to acquire that position.

If, after you are hired, you reasonably believe that your contributions are substantial and of value to your employer, do not let anyone marginalize you and your efforts. Executives who have been labeled A, B, and C players in one company have gone on to achieve huge success as A players in much more successful, respected, and highly regarded companies.

As an employee, if your supervisor has not told you how you are performing, ask him or her. You need to know in order to plan your employment strategy and future. Ask for suggestions for improvement. This shows that you really want to succeed.

Family and friends are a different matter. Depending on the quality of your personal and professional support network, you may need to marshal the strength to repel and distance yourself from detractors. If they are "friends," find new ones. If they are family members, interact with them less frequently.

Do not be swayed by what others think and believe is important unless you respect their opinions. Even then, gather more data. Contact others whose opinions you respect, such as a former teacher, coach, professor, supervisor, or anyone who has demonstrated sound judgment. Ask them what they think about your goals, given what they know about you.

The person whose opinion you seek should either have specific or generic experience in the business or profession of interest to you or be someone who can obtain feedback for you from someone who does.

You will likely get from your employment search what you put into it in terms of, among other things, time, effort, follow-up, networking, job-board searches, and résumé preparation. Persistence and tenacity are essential to achieving positive results; without them, you will not likely be successful.

If the data gathered support the conclusion that you are average or not likely to be successful in the role you envision for yourself, consider whether to redirect your efforts. If you feel strongly and passionately about your career selection, do not give up your dreams and goals because of naysayers. After a reasonable period, reevaluate your decision.

**TIP 1-17 Find inspiration from other people's journeys and successes.**
Athletes, entertainers, and chefs have stories of overcoming poverty, abandonment, physical and substance abuse, and other challenges. Their recital of how far they have come and how their sport and craft saved them evokes awe, respect, and inspiration. These stories of struggle, redemption, self-reflection, and vindication are worth your time.

Watch ESPN programming for heartrending stories of athletes' survival in the face of overwhelmingly dire circumstances. Similarly, the Food Network's *Chopped* often includes short interviews in which chefs share the obstacles that they climbed over to reach their spot on the show.

You do not have to like sports or cooking shows to benefit from the experience of watching the programming. It can be a sobering experience, but one which may invigorate and propel you forward with new momentum. If those athletes, entertainers, and chefs can do it, so can you.

For inspiration, either read Liz Murray's biography online or watch the Lifetime movie, *Homeless to Harvard: The Liz Murray Story*. Amanda Kloots's decision to take charge of her life and career after the rejections and unexpected unemployment associated with being an actor is also instructive. [14] Regardless of your gender or gender expression, these stories should inspire you.

**TIP 1-18 Consider all feedback a gift.**

---

[14] Kloots, A. 2018. "How I Overcame Losing My Job and Marriage—With a Jump Rope." *TIME*, May 3, 2018, https://time.com/5262866/overcoming-divorce-job-loss/

**TIP 1-19 Accept negative feedback without becoming defensive.**
Constructive feedback almost always includes both positive and negative information, some of which you may agree with and some you may not. If you elicit feedback, be sure to accept it graciously, even if you do not agree with it.

Accept it as you would accept an ugly gift from a loved one. Consider it a gift, one that makes you smile, because it will help you improve.

At the very least, feedback may give you information about the person who gives it. If you thought the person was a supporter, the feedback provided may change your mind.

If you do not receive negative feedback well, you need to practice. How well you handle feedback may be a factor when recruiters debrief you after an interview and/or when your supervisor gives you your annual performance review.

A few words of caution are appropriate. People considered supporters may not show it in their feedback. Others might be more generous with positive feedback than expected.

Before concluding that people who only give negative feedback are not supportive, consider whether they have experience giving feedback. Do they know that constructive feedback is generally delivered by giving positive comments first followed by less favorable, more temperate comments? You may want to confirm that they know this before judging them too harshly, especially if they are friends.

Depending on the circumstances, it may be prudent to ask several potential feedback providers to give you constructive feedback. This information may contribute to your personal and professional development.

**TIP 1-20 Do not shoot the messenger.**
Like feedback, information received during a job search or at work may be positive or negative. It may be conveyed by someone who may or may not know you well or like you. Human resources ("HR") employees and a former supervisor, coach, or professor are examples of possible sources.

Regardless, do not react negatively toward the person who delivers the message or information. It is simply bad form. Furthermore, that person may be someone you will meet again, and he or she may recall—to your detriment—how you handled yourself.

### TIP 1-21 Maintain a positive attitude.

Simply put, no one wants to help a person with a bad attitude.

*Nicole did not graduate from college and did not get good grades in high school, but she acquired additional training after high school. Somehow Nicole always finds a job. She has changed jobs several times for personal reasons and each time she needed to find another job, someone hired her.*

*Why? Nicole's references are effusive in their praise of her interpersonal relationship skills, work ethic, and reliability. People consistently describe her as having "a nice way about her." She always has a smile, never has a negative attitude, works hard, does her job well, and is always on time for work. Nicole is someone to emulate.*

### TIP 1-22 Follow sound advice unless you have a good reason to do otherwise.

You will probably receive advice from many different people some who know what they are talking about and others not so much. Do not forget to exercise due diligence to determine whether the advice given by others works for you and your situation. That is, before you decide, objectively check the reliability and suitability of your source.

Questions you might ask yourself include the following: What do you know about the person? Is he successful by your standards? Does she have the background—that is, education and work experience—that makes her knowledgeable?

If you do not know the person offering advice, check out his or her bona fides or credentials to confirm that the advice offered at least has some credible basis to justify your consideration. Beware of those who claim to have all the answers. If possible, look for breadth and depth of experience and increasing levels of responsibility possessed by individuals who offer advice.

### TIP 1-23 Seek information, not affirmation.

Unbiased information is powerful. If nothing else, it enables you to make informed decisions. Regardless of the type of job you seek, you need objective feedback about who people think you are and the value you can bring to an employer. Family and friends are not objective about you and your talents. Input from an eclectic group of people you can rely on to give you constructive feedback is not only important, it is essential.

If you can, find people of various ages, ethnicities, religions, and sexual expressions, along with professionals employed in a multitude of functions. The individuals you select should know you well enough to be helpful as you plan your career.

At work, vary your lunch and break friends to include people in other departments and offices within the company to obtain a broader view. You may have to introduce yourself to individuals you do not know, but the possible advantages may enhance your employment experience. At the very least, you will expand your network of contacts.

If you cannot amass such a group, do the best you can with the people you know. Going forward, your efforts to expand your network base and make it as varied as possible will benefit you.

**TIP 1-24 Develop and maintain relationships thoughtfully and wisely.** In Chapter 5, you are going to be asked to think about who will accompany you on your employment journey. Go ahead and begin a mental list of loved ones, friends, family members, coaches, instructors, and the other people you know whom you might include on your list, and why. Ideally, this list will be the start of a network that will grow and serve you well in the future.

*Persevere*

**TIP 1-25 Do not give up or give in.**

> *When the world says, "Give up," Hope whispers, "Try it one more time."*
>
> —Author unknown

If your lack of success finding a job or receiving a promotion makes you feel underappreciated by prospective employers or ignored by your supervisor despite your marketable skills, conduct a reality check.

Ask yourself: Have I

- Exhausted all possible avenues that could lead me to success?
- Been more flexible than I have ever been?
- Stepped outside of my comfort zone?
- Engaged in introspective reflection to identify areas that may need improvement?

Even if you are satisfied that the answers to all these questions are "yes," and you believe that you are close to success, you are likely to realize that this journey you are now on can be humbling.

Do not let anyone tell you that you cannot or should not achieve your goals. Do not give up or give in to your emotional ups and downs. Stay the course ... press on. Failure (at least on a permanent basis) is not an option.

## Resources

### Mindset

- National Alliance on Mental Illness (NAMI) is a national grassroots mental illness organization that provides education, advocacy and other support to individuals affected by mental illness. https://nami.org/Home
- Substance Abuse and Mental Health Services Administration (SAMHSA) https://samhsa.gov/
- Thrive Global, https://thriveglobal.com/categories/community/
- The Holistic Root to Managing Anxiety by Maria Tabone https://amazon.com/Holistic-Root-Managing-Anxiety/dp/0615356222
- The Resiliency Advantage: Master Change, Thrive Under Pressure, and Bounce
- Back from Setbacks by Al Siebert https://amazon.com/Resiliency-Advantage-Master-Pressure-Setbacks/dp/1576753298
- 10 Signs of an Ailing Mind, Colette Bouchez, June 28, 2007. https://samigroup.blogspot.com/2007/06/10-signs-of-ailing-mind.html
- How to cope with feeling stressed and overwhelmed, Rachael Roberts, February 27, 2019. https://life-resourceful.com/2019/02/27/dealing-with-stress-and-overwhelm/
- Warning Signs of Mental Illness, Physician Review, Ranna Parekh, M.D., M.P.H., July 2018. https://psychiatry.org/patients-families/warning-signs-ofmental-illness

- How to Cope When You Constantly Feel Overwhelmed, by Maureen Campaiola, August 2. 2020. https://adebtfreestressfreelife.com/feel-overwhelmed/
- What to Do When You Feel Overwhelmed, Sara Young Wang July 19, 2018. https://forbes.com/sites/sarayoungwang/2018/07/19/what-to-do-when-youfeel-overwhelmed/#74bfcbd56c6a
- 7 Ways to Cope When You Feel Overwhelmed, by Toria Sheffield, November 6, 2015, https://bustle.com/articles/122091-7-ways-to-cope-when-you-feel-overwhelmed

## *Meditation*

- 6 Great Online Tools to Help You Meditate, https://inc.com/john-boitnott/6-online-tools-to-help-entrepreneurs-meditate.html
- 7 Powerful Meditation Tools to Help You Train Your Mind, https://scottjeffrey.com/best-meditation-tools/
- The 10 Best Meditation Tools: Unlocking The Sacred Wisdom https://yourbodythetemple.com/best-meditation-tools/

## *Exercise*

- A selection of exercise videos, Bing https://bing.com/search?q=exercise+videos
- How to Train Like an Olympic Athlete and Get Results, Paige Waehner, https://verywellfit.com/train-like-an-olympic-athlete-1231196

# CHAPTER 2

# Inconvenient Truths

*How would your life be different if ... you stopped worrying about things you can't control and started focusing on the things you can?*
—Steve Maraboli, speaker, author,
personal coach, and national radio show host

## Reflections

Creating multiple revenue streams, turning a passion into a revenue-generating venture, and reinventing, rebranding, or redirecting themselves are examples of how creative people can be in trying times.

**TIP 2-26 Individuals in pursuit of employment will need to be more flexible, creative, and technologically savvy.**
Technological innovation, among other things, has changed the way business is conducted. Relationships are still important, but there has been a shift from doing business face to face through established relationships to handling matters remotely with the emphasis on cost effectiveness.

Business and human innovation[1] and artificial intelligence disrupt traditional or conventional ways of conducting business. Human resources departments now use analytics to predict and identify future outcomes.

---

[1] Martinuzzi, B. 2019. "American Express' Blog." *Business Innovation: How Artificial Intelligence Is Changing Business,* May 23, 2019. https://american-express.com/en-us/business/trends-and-insights/articles/business-innovation—how-artificial-intelligence-is-changing-business/ Breakstone, M. 2019. *Three Ways Artificial Intelligence Can Drive Human Innovation,* March 6, 2019; https://forbes.com/sites/forbestechcouncil/2019/03/06/three-ways-artificial-intelligencecan-drive-human-innovation

Core traits to look for in applicants for employment, employee retention, and turnover are a few of the areas in which HR uses predictive analytics.[2]

Particularly during a skilled labor shortage, more precise predictions—and therefore, decisions—are important. Reportedly, the best candidates do not stay on the job market long before getting snapped up. Furthermore, people are job-hopping more than ever before.[3]

Monitoring industry trends, business performance, and technological developments are essential to keeping informed and woke.

**TIP 2-27 Finding a job requires work, focus, and effort.**

Wanting and needing a job will not get you hired. Identify the geographical locations where there are available jobs and where there are the most jobs in the largest area within commuting distance. There is more to be done, such as scouring job boards; initiating and participating in networking

---

[2] White, D. 2019. "'Tech Funnel' Blog." *Top 3 Examples of Predictive Analytics in HR,* June 5, 2019, https://techfunnel.com/hr-tech/top-3-examples-of-predictiveanalytics-in-hr/

[3] Davies, R. 2019. "'Software Advice' Blog." *How Recruiters Can Use Predictive Analytics To Improve Hiring,* October 2, 2019, https://softwareadvice.com/resources/predictive-analytics-recruitment-hiring/

activities; drafting different versions of your résumé, marketing pitches, and cover and thank you letters; and practicing interviewing skills.

You will need to research the industry in which you are interested in working. Determine which materials you will submit and in what format and the clothing you will wear for interviews. Depending on the business culture, submissions and clothing may be different for corporate, creative, building trades, public sector, or nonprofit employment opportunities.

**TIP 2-28 Your employment matters are solely your responsibility.**
In the New Employment Reality, individuals cannot rely on anyone else to chart the courses of their careers. Everyday people, who do not have the leverage that professional athletes have, still have options. Once they determine the career path that fits them best, they should set a course for success as they define it and work toward that goal.

There may be periods of unemployment but, by turning a passion, hobby, or interest into an income stream, people can earn money. A temporary or part-time job is another way to make money while searching for full-time employment. Depending on business needs and the person's performance, this option has the additional benefit of possibly evolving into a full-time position. A paid or unpaid internship is another option that can evolve into a full-time job offer.

*Recently laid off from his music business manager position, due to the lack of interest in his résumé, Vin decided to pursue another line of work. Through his research he identified a demand for art and art education in public television and a void in the marketplace for that programming.*

*Vin's lack of formal production training did not deter him. He learned by doing, researching, and collaborating. He brought in others who had experience that he did not have at the time. By enlisting the talents of those who had expertise he lacked, Vin increased his skill and knowledge.*

*Now a documentary film producer, Vin says if you find yourself unemployed, find a job you can make money at and follow your dream while working. By sticking it out at his first job, Vin was able to make connections that led to his dream job.*

*You can find Vin's PBS documentary series The Hudson River School, parts 1 and 2, on Amazon Prime or ShopPBS.org and his podcast interview at https://youremploymentmatters. com/podcast/.*

Each day, a tremendous number of people vie for a limited number of jobs that did not exist 15 to 20 years ago. Consequently, be loyal to and trust yourself. Today, anyone looking for work or aspiring toward promotion should:

- Use all available resources aggressively and exhaustively;
- Take nothing for granted;
- Dispel any feelings of entitlement;
- Keep up their spirits; and
- Maintain a sense of humor.

## TIP 2-29 You do not know what you do not know and why you do not know it.

This may sound like double talk, but it is not. Often in a work environment, information is disseminated in measured doses on a need-to-know basis.

For example, a bonus plan may be a component of your supervisor's compensation package. There are probably objectives or goals identified and target metrics tied to how much the supervisor's bonus payout will be.

Under the bonus plan, the better your supervisor performs against the goals, the higher the bonus payout. If there is no bonus plan, there are likely target goals. The supervisor's performance review rating is likely tied to the quality and quantity of the goals met.

Individual employee and team performance on projects can adversely impact a supervisor's performance objectives and bonus payout. If an employee or team of employees fails to perform well on such projects, the supervisor may lose bonus money or receive a negative rating on his or her performance review.

As a direct report, your objective is to perform at a high level and to make your supervisor look good. Your performance review, if you receive one, should reflect your stellar performance.

You may not be bonus eligible, but benefits should filter down from your supervisor to you. If you do not receive a performance review, ask to meet with your supervisor to discuss your performance.

Ask how you are performing, what more you could have done to receive a better evaluation, what you can do to improve and move to the next level. Follow up with an e-mail thanking the supervisor for meeting with you to discuss how you are performing.

Remember: No matter how talented you are, how gifted you may be, or how brilliant you have been told you are, you will not be privy to information that, for example, is above your position or pay grade.

### TIP 2-30 "Job security" is a contradiction in terms.

Economic downturns shift the focus, albeit briefly, from the high rate of unemployment to what happened to the lost jobs. Substantial loss of jobs through business strategies such as restructuring, right-sizing, outsourcing, and off-shoring is controversial.

In the aftermath, work previously performed by permanent, full-time employees is now performed by a cadre of temporary or gig workers or independent contractors. Businesses that formerly operated domestically have moved, at least some operations, to foreign locations.

Consequently, long years of service are not easy to achieve today and provide little if any job security. Long-term employees who have been laid off and are unable to find comparable work are acutely aware that the employment landscape has changed. By comparison, people who are employed and have not otherwise been adversely impacted by the shift in the employment picture breathe a sigh of relief because they dodged a bullet—at least for the time being.

### TIP 2-31 You are not better than anyone, and no one is better than you.

If you have never been told that you are special or been made to feel that you are, then begin by embracing the truth that you are not better than anyone else and no one is better than you are.

Regardless of how you view yourself, it is important that "respect" be your touchstone in the employment environment and elsewhere. It should be a permanent element of your personal brand. Respect for yourself, others, and the company or business for which you work or want to work are prerequisites for success in the workplace.

- Always speak to coworkers in a respectful tone, regardless of level, title, position, or whether you like them.
- Require the same in return.

- Do not let your ego make you think you are better than someone because it gets you nowhere and only makes you look insecure.

It is not a one-way street. Rather, it is a mutual understanding and agreement to conduct oneself civilly, professionally, and politely. A smile, a hello, or some other cordial greeting can help the person properly classify you as a confident, competent applicant or worker, who understands the meaning of R-E-S-P-E-C-T. Conduct yourself in a manner that reflects your personal regard for yourself and others.

Do not make the mistake of becoming too familiar and too comfortable with your supervisor and other employees in higher positions. It is wise to maintain a level of professionalism and self-respect. Someone will notice.

You never know when you will have an opportunity to present yourself and your career goals to someone who can help you or knows someone who can. That said, you should always be "on" and bring your "A" game so that you recognize and take advantage of an opportunity when it appears. It may not come again.

*Dorly worked at a major corporation. At an event for a senior executive who was leaving the company, Dorly introduced himself to the departing executive and wished him well as he pursued future endeavors.*

*The executive asked Dorly how he had worked on his team for four months, yet the executive did not know his name. Dorly explained that he had not had the opportunity to meet him.*

*Taking Dorly aside, the executive corrected him. He told Dorly that in the previous four months, Dorly had never stepped outside his comfort zone to introduce himself. According to Dorly, that lesson will stick with him forever.*[4]

**TIP 2-32 To your loved ones, you may be all that and a bag of "chips" but, in the workplace, you are an applicant, employee, and a coworker.** Depending on how involved your loved ones are in the different aspects of your life, you may have to have a polite but firm conversation with

---

[4] Bouguignon, D. 2020. "Your Employment Matters with Beverly Williams." Podcast, *How to Step Outside Your Comfort Zone,* https://youremployment-matters.com/podcast

them. As much as they want to help, they are likely looking at you through rose-colored glasses. They also might not know when to interfere and when to step aside. If you decide to have a talk with them, you should:

- Acknowledge their love and good intentions.
- Assure them that you need their help to make networking contacts, practice your marketing pitch to prospective employers, and prepare for interviews.
- Tell them that, if you do not follow their advice, this does not mean that you do not appreciate or respect it.

**TIP 2-33 Your family members are not always right, but they are not always wrong.**

*Carolyn, who has a Master of Business Administration (MBA) from a prestigious business school, did not give her son the appropriate advice. Carolyn's son James is a junior in college who wants to pursue a career as a sportswriter.*

*Through his networking contacts, James was given a courtesy interview with Jonah, a sportswriter with an online column and blog. James appropriately planned to send Jonah an e-mail to thank him for his time and the information he provided. Carolyn was appalled. She directed James to purchase a card so that he could send a handwritten thank you via snail mail.*

The type of thank you depends on the person to whom you are sending it. Online columnists and bloggers are digital people. An e-mail thank you or e-card is acceptable and may be preferred by people like Jonah who work remotely and communicate electronically. James was right. Although Carolyn's intentions were good, and a thank you note was appropriate, her advice was wrong given the circumstances.

*Rosa and her husband Javier planned to attend a social event hosted by Javier's manager at a local restaurant, but Rosa had a job interview the afternoon of the event. To save time, Javier said that he would drive her to the job interview and wait for her in the reception area.*

*Javier was correct to want to save time, but Rosa knew that, if her well-meaning husband accompanied her to the interview, it would appear unprofessional and inappropriate. Rosa gently yet firmly explained this to Javier and suggested that he wait for her at a nearby coffee shop.*

Even if your social media network is robust, it will not hurt to sit down with your family and come up with a list of all the people in your combined networks.

**TIP 2-34 It is your employer's "party", and you are an invited guest.**
In the absence of a contract or other legal instrument or a violation of law, generally, employers have the right to discharge employees with or without a good reason. In this situation, individuals are employed at will. The "at-will" category covers employees who are not protected by express or implied employment contracts.

No matter what anyone tells you, absent a violation of law, usually it is your employer's party, and you are merely an invited guest, but there is good news and bad news. The bad news is that unless there are extenuating circumstances (often legal), your employer may discharge you at any time. The good news is that you can resign at any time, although it is customary to give two weeks' notice.

**TIP 2-35 Consider whether to avoid discussions about religion, politics, sex, health problems, issues with loved ones, and your career aspirations.**
In democratic countries, freedom of speech may be a fundamental right. Although you may have a right to make a statement, be prepared to be judged fairly or unfairly about what you say. There are topics and viewpoints that may cause people to draw conclusions accurately or inaccurately about your character and intelligence.

Religion, politics, sex (particularly your sex life), your health problems, problems with loved ones, and your career aspirations are examples of such topics. Consequently, seriously consider whether to share your opinions, your personal practices and situations, and your future employment aspirations with your supervisors and coworkers.

These management employees, who may appear to be open-minded and "with it," may instead be less "with it" and more judgmental than you know. More importantly, you do not want your boss to think that you are "high maintenance" or that you have too much drama in your life, and thus are not committed to your job. At the very least, these behaviors may negatively influence your employer's opinion of you.

Most people will not ask for whom you voted, whether you go to church or how you worship, or why you went to the doctor. Just in case, though, you should be prepared with a response that firmly yet politely does not disclose much about your opinions, beliefs, and experiences.

- If you decide to engage coworkers and supervisors in discussions about these topics:
  - Conduct yourself civilly and professionally.
  - Prepare to hear opposing viewpoints.
  - Recognize that
    i People form opinions based on personal interactions.
    ii Everyone does not acquire information from the same or accurate sources.
- If asked to identify a political party affiliation, you may respond that you try to keep up with both sides of the issues and vote for the candidate that you believe is most closely aligned with your views.
- When asked about your career goals, consider saying that you are interested in moving up, but right now (especially if you just joined the company) you want to help the company be successful by being the best team player you can be.

**Do not get it twisted:** If your supervisor asks you what your future goals and ambitions are, you must discuss them. To avoid the appearance of disloyalty, articulate your ambitions in terms of your current employer to avoid any conclusions that you will leave when a better job comes along.

Realize that how you handle these discussions may affect your career now and in the future. Given the possible career-limiting implications, ask yourself if this is the hill you want to die on. If the answer is "yes," climb the hill.

**TIP 2-36 Avoid conduct that may result in negative media coverage unless you are committed to your cause.**

Examples of career-limiting or inappropriate behavior include:

- Unprofessional, rude, or obscene conduct
- Drunkenness
- Disorderly or criminal activity on the job or in public

The rule of thumb is "Do not do anything you would not want to read about on the front page of *The New York Times* or *The Wall Street Journal*," after which your loved ones would ask, "What were you thinking?" In other words, do not embarrass yourself or the people important to you. Negative, adverse media coverage may place in jeopardy your continued employment with your current and future employers.

**TIP 2-37 Do not let your ego get in the way. If you do not know, say so.**
Regardless of where you are in your career, you are not likely to know how to do everything you will be asked to do or be able to answer every question you are asked. If you are looking for employment, you should anticipate questions that might be asked as you network and interview and practice your responses.

If you are employed, anticipate questions that might come up in the discussion or presentation, and be prepared with answers and information. If the questions do not come up and you think the material you have is relevant and helpful, include the information in a question. You can then explain why the information you have is relevant to the discussion.

**TIP 2-38 Your habits, behaviors, opinions, and social mores may be endearing to your friends and family but not to your employer.**
Unfortunately, identifying the characteristics that may need to be changed may require that you elicit feedback that may be difficult for you to hear. To find a job and be successful on the job once you are hired, set aside these characteristics. At the very least, reevaluate them.

Remember to consider feedback a gift and do not become defensive. It is counterproductive.

# CHAPTER 3

# Networking Is the GPS to Employment Success

*Reveal not every secret you have to a friend, for how*
*can you tell but that friend may hereafter become an*
*enemy. And bring not all mischief you are able to upon*
*an enemy, for he may one day become your friend.*
                          —Saadi Shirazi, poet (1184 to 1291)

*Networking remains the No. 1 cause of job attainment.*
                          —Hal Lancaster, author, and editor

# Reflections

*Even rock stars realize the benefits of networking, taking advantage of opportunities and having multiple income streams. Sean Huber is the drummer of Philadelphia's punk rock/indie band Modern Baseball and two-piece punk/rock band Vicky Speedboat as well as singer/songwriter for Steady Hands. Sean graduated from Drexel University and then began a national tour with Modern Baseball. For the last few years, Sean has been working full time as a sales representative and more recently a Mid Atlantic Territory sales manager for Two Roads Brewing Company.*[1]

# Social What?

Social media is a great tool. By all means, use Instagram, Twitter, and Facebook, as well as texting and any other means of communication that connects you with people and allows you to tell them that you need their help to find a job. Your use, however, should not be detrimental to your efforts to secure employment.

In the United States, freedom of speech is a constitutionally protected right, but there are limitations on the exercise of the right. Furthermore, even if the speech or conduct is protected, there may be consequences, including denial or loss of employment.

**TIP 3-39 Use social media wisely.**
It is no secret that some employers use social media to screen prospective employees. According to one source, 90 percent of employers review job applicants' social media profiles.[2] The same source reports that 79 percent

---

[1] Huber, S. 2020. "Your Employment Matters with Beverly Williams Podcast." *The Rock Star and Following Your Dream,* 2020, https://youremploymentmatters.com/podcast

[2] Rathore, S. 2020. "90% of Employers Consider an Applicant's Social Media Activity During Hiring Process." May 5, 2020. https://smallbiztrends.com/2020/05/social-media-screening.html; McKeon, K. 2020. "The Manifest' Blog 5 Personal Branding Tips for Your Job Search." April 28, 2020, https://themanifest.com/digital-marketing/5-personal-branding-tips-job-search

of businesses have rejected applicants because of their social media content. [3]

Friends and other contacts may search for you on Google or look you up on Instagram or LinkedIn before they refer you. Consequently, you want to make sure that you do not have anything on social media sites that is detrimental to your efforts.

All job-search materials you post on social media platforms of any kind must be accurate, consistent with similar materials found elsewhere, and convey professionalism. If the material you have posted is controversial, unflattering, or does not otherwise meet these requirements, remove the material from your social networking sites. Do not rely on privacy settings.

**LinkedIn:** LinkedIn is primarily a business site used by recruiters and job seekers.[4] It is a place to look up people and companies by name, geographical area, and location or college. Always keep your profile updated so recruiters and former colleagues can connect with you.

If you decide to create a LinkedIn profile, be careful. Your LinkedIn profile is (or should be) a short version of your résumé. Make sure the two are consistent. LinkedIn is a tool you may use in several different ways:

- To get your information to recruiters who will search the www.linkedin.com database.
- To look up information about the people who will interview you. For example, if you know that you will be interviewing with Jane Doe of the ABC Company, you can look up Jane Doe on LinkedIn, and then review whatever is posted about her. It may be a short bio or a synopsis of work experience and education.
- To connect with classmates, colleagues, and contacts.
- To reach out and establish a connection, which may lead to connections with people through a second or third source.

Sites like LinkedIn and Glassdoor are great tools to find out about businesses you are interested in working for and what is going on in those businesses.

---

[3] Ibid.

[4] How to Use LinkedIn Effectively, Alison Doyle, The Balance Careers, March 5, 2020, https://thebalancecareers.com/how-to-use-linkedin-2062597

Whatever you do, make sure that your digital footprint is scrubbed. Monitor it regularly to be sure it remains that way. Do not post inappropriate statuses or pictures under any circumstances, particularly if you are friends with coworkers.

- Even though there should be a line between work life and personal life, do not assume it is normal to share everything with coworkers.
- Revise your settings accordingly if you are friends with coworkers and want a certain level of privacy.
- Keep in mind that passwords and privacy settings do not always work effectively.

**TIP 3-40 Make sure you understand the scope and breadth of the meaning of networking and social networking and the implications.**

**Social networking:** To paraphrase Merriam-Webster, "networking" is the exchange of information, data, or services among people as individuals or in groups or institutions, particularly to cultivate and further productive employment or business relationships.[5] By comparison, "social networking" is defined by the same source as "the creation and maintenance of personal and business relationships, especially online."[6]

---

[5] "Networking." Merriam-Webster.com Dictionary, Merriam-Webster, https://merriam-webster.com/dictionary/networking, (accessed on August 17, 2020).

[6] Ibid.

"According to most experts, networking is building relationships on the basis of trust that involves a give and take.... Networking is not optional anymore; it is a crucial skill to master."[7]

Significantly, the foregoing definitions include references to "employment," "business," and "workplace." By some accounts, approximately 70 percent of employers use Facebook to screen prospective employees.[8] Think about that before you post sexually explicit, provocative pictures or exchanges that contain inappropriate or questionable language, references, or statements that may come back to haunt you.

"Tell-All Generation Learns to Keep Things Offline"[9] speaks to anyone who is social network obsessed and texts, posts, and tweets without an eye to the future. Issues of privacy aside, "[s]ocial networking requires vigilance, not only in what you post, but what your friends post about you."[10]

The article describes individuals under 30 who began sharing their lives and opinions on social networks as teenagers but who, as adults, wish they had censored themselves more and shared less.[11] If you do not know what conduct is inappropriate or questionable, ask yourself, "If this behavior was pictured or described on a news website or on the nightly newscast, would my grandmother be embarrassed?"

---

[7] Rangwala, S. 2012. "Networking 101, Build Relationships and Advance in Your Career." *The Washington Post,* October 9, 2012, https://washingtonpost.com/jobs_articles/2012/10/09/dbb7d628-121d-11e2-be82-c3411b7680a9_story.html

[8] Salm, L. 2017. "70% of Employers are Snooping Candidates' Social Media Profiles." Blog, *CareerBuilder* June 15, 2017, https://careerbuilder.com/advice/social-media-survey-2017

[9] Holson, L.M. 2010. "Tell-All Generation Learns to Keep Things Offline." *The New York Times,* May 10, 2010. https://privacylives.com/new-york-times-tell-allgeneration-learns-to-keep-things-offline/2010/05/10/

[10] Ibid., quoting Mary Madden, a senior research specialist who oversaw a Pew study that examined online behavior.

[11] In truth, adults are as addicted to Facebook and other social media sites as the Tell-All Generation. The ease with which information can be shared with "friends" and loved ones, including highlights of family events, permits people to connect and remain connected whether they are near or far away.

**TIP 3-41 Consider the possible long-term consequences before you post material on social networking sites.**
Whether you are young or older, you have a future ahead. You may think that you can do whatever you want now. Think again. Think about the consequences.

Picture the facial expression on the person who was about to offer you the job of your dreams—the supervisor who was going to become your boss, or your current boss who was considering you for promotion. What are they looking at? He or she sees the spring-break photos or the "love" video you and the person you thought you were going to marry posted on a social media platform.

Here is some of the online conduct to avoid as enumerated in "15 Career-Killing Facebook Mistakes":

1. Inappropriate pictures
2. Complaining about your current job and supervisor
3. Posting information that conflicts with your résumé
4. Posting status updates you do not want your boss or coworkers to see
5. Not understanding your security settings
6. Revealing personal information[12]

A thorough review of the article is worthwhile. Posting provocative material that may adversely affect or limit your employment opportunities may have other unintended consequences.

**Note:** Transmitting sexually graphic pictures of underage individuals, even with their consent, may violate child pornography laws, which could lead to criminal prosecution.

**TIP 3-42 If you "friend" a coworker, be sure not to post anything that might be used against you to damage your reputation at work.**
Current friends with access to your page or site may inadvertently or jokingly disclose sensitive material, or in the future become "frenemies" or even outright enemies. As you know, romances and friendships do not

---

[12] Reddy, K. "15 Career-Killing Facebook Mistakes." https://content.wisestep. com/career-killing-facebook-mistakes-you-must-know/

always end on amicable terms. Making sound decisions now will allow you to have more options in the future.

**A picture is worth a thousand words:**
Sexting, love-making films, and vacation frivolity—such as baring it all in front of a camera—may seem harmless, especially if your judgment is impaired by alcohol, drugs, or medication, but there are risks.

- Proceed with caution.
- Be discreet.
- What you do behind closed doors is your business, but it is risky to record or otherwise preserve private, especially sexually explicit, photos.

Consider this scenario:
*Theresa complained that June, her supervisor, did not like her because Theresa is an atheist. She also complained that June induced a coworker named Albert, who also reported to June, to sexually harass Theresa. Her employer initiated an internal investigation to determine whether Theresa's allegations had merit.*

*To prove her allegation of sexual harassment, Theresa produced a sexually graphic picture of Albert that he had sexted her. When Albert was questioned, he laughed. He said, among other things, he and Theresa had a consensual sexual relationship, and he could prove it. Albert forwarded a nude picture of Theresa that she had sent him.*

Theresa was discharged because she had filed a bogus complaint. That is but one lesson. Imagine how you would feel if intimate pictures of you were circulated in the workplace, even on a limited basis.

**Technology:** Technology has revolutionized social networking. Do not forget, however, that electronic and paper record trails can follow you indefinitely. The commonly held belief that information, communications, and pictures posted on social media and transmitted by computers, cell phones, and other technology are accessible only to individuals selected and approved by the page owner is simply incorrect.

- Review your page often, even daily, while you are searching for employment.

- You may be judged by the company you keep, as indicated by the material on your page.

It is up to you to make sure that any material, such as provocative pictures and language from "friends," which cast you in an unfavorable light, is removed from your page before they can do any harm to your efforts to find a job.

**Twitter:** Tweeting after an interview, boasting about how awesomely you performed, including negative comments about the interviewers, or calling into question their intellect because they bought your "act" or you "got one over on them" is a bad idea.

If somehow an interviewer sees the tweet, you can kiss your dream job goodbye. Likewise, derogatory, or otherwise uncomplimentary tweets about your employer, supervisor, or coworkers can have a career-limiting effect.

Whether you are employed or seeking employment, imagine that, down the road years from now, you become a parent, and you are being considered for a high-level position with a company, or the president of the United States offers you a cabinet post. What will you say to your loved ones, particularly your children, when the forgotten images of your youth are shown?

To avoid the experience, forego immediate gratification and the knee-jerk temptation to communicate and otherwise share the first thought that comes to mind as well as controversial pictures you would not want shared with the world.

Ask yourself, "Is it worth it?" Let me answer for you: "No!"

**Privacy:** You may be entitled to privacy, but your privacy is not guaranteed. Furthermore, social networks may start out with strong privacy policies, but those policies may change over time for financial reasons or change in leadership without your knowledge. If you are not sure you are making the right decision, ask someone whose opinion you respect. The person should have a proven record of staying out of trouble and a solid reputation.

To summarize, early in life you may not consider your conduct indiscreet and inappropriate; later in life, you probably will.

- Workplace relationships that go bad, such as a friendship or a love affair, can have career-limiting consequences.

- "Live" inappropriate behavior and sexually graphic or otherwise provocative pictures and communications posted on social networks should be avoided at all costs.

### (Old-school and new-school) networking

**TIP 3-43 It is a high-tech world, but do not forget the human factor.**

**TIP 3-44 Tell trustworthy people you know, and those you have recently met that you are looking for a job and you need their help.** Many, if not most, people get jobs through networking.[13] There are great stories about people getting job leads from unexpected places.

*1. Alexis knew that she wanted to work for a magazine. She and a college friend heard that Teen Vogue was hosting an event in New York City. Deciding not to pass up a networking opportunity, Alexis and her friend went into action. They spoke to their professor to get excused from class, had business cards printed at Staples, and hopped on a Greyhound bus for the seven-hour ride from Syracuse to New York City.[14]*

*2. Two coworkers, who were employed as compensation professionals at an energy company, were miserable in their jobs. They had joined the company around the same time, and both lamented their decision to accept positions with the company. One of the workers could not take it any longer and resigned after 18 months, leaving his colleague behind, but they kept in touch.*

*One day, the employee who was left behind received a call from another employer, inviting her to come for an interview. At first, she did not understand because she had not applied for a job with this company. To her surprise, she found out that she had been referred by her former colleague, who had been offered the job but turned it down. Within four weeks of her interview, she received a job offer, which she happily accepted.*

---

[13] "Networking." Merriam-Webster.com Dictionary, *Merriam Webster* quoting Hal Lancaster, https://merriam-webster.com/dictionary/networking, (accessed on August 17, 2020).

[14] Jones, A. 2020. "Your Employment Matters with Beverly Williams Podcast." *How to Stand Out and Get Noticed at Work,* https://youremploymentmatters.com/podcast/

The story below is not technically networking but rather the result of an applicant's powerful interview and the positive impression she made on a prospective employer.

*A woman applied for a position with a prominent pharmaceutical company. The interview with the manager went extremely well, so the candidate was disappointed when the manager informed her that she had not been selected for the position.*

*This highly regarded company would have represented a significant coup for future employment opportunities if she had been hired and could include it on her résumé. The manager asked her, however, if she would consider another position if one became available. Of course, the candidate said yes.*

*About five or six weeks later, the former candidate received a call from the manager. She was excited to think that another opportunity with the pharmaceutical company had become available. Although she hoped to receive a job offer, she was somewhat leery that there was another vacancy within the department so soon.*

*As it turned out, the manager was calling to offer her a position not at the pharmaceutical company but at the corporate headquarters of a much larger, global organization. The manager had left the pharmaceutical company but remembered the former candidate.*

*They met for lunch after her call, during which the manager described the job and told the woman that the position, should she choose to accept it, was hers.*

These scenarios illustrate (1) the importance of being the person that a former coworker would recommend for a job that they turned down; and (2) being so impressive during an interview that the interviewer remembers you favorably and offers to hire you at a later date. If you make a commitment to do the necessary work, you too can become the person others think of when they are asked if they know anyone they can recommend.

One way to maximize the likelihood that favorable job-search results will be achieved is to embrace both old-school and new-school networking. Both methods should be used simultaneously and vigorously to achieve employment success. To use an old-school phrase, "Leave no stone unturned."

The new-school approach to almost everything in this high-tech world is to rely on social networking for everything, from looking for a job to communicating thoughts, ideas, hopes, and dreams.

If you are new school:

- You may feel that you should have a job simply because you graduated from college, or because you want or need one; and
- You focus primarily (if not exclusively) on Internet-based job boards for employment opportunities.

If you have this mindset, you will be surprised when you are not contacted for an interview, especially when you have followed up and followed up and followed up. Apparently, you did not get the text message or e-mail, which informed you that in this new-school, high-tech, electronic world, there is simply no substitute for old-school, "live," person-to-person contact. This method of networking, especially through referrals and recommendations, can almost magically get a person in the door for at least an exploratory or courtesy interview.

The reasons are simple. Given the number of talented, educated, skilled people who are looking for work, hiring decisions, especially those made in a challenging economy, will be based in part on intangibles.

These decisions will also be driven by first impressions based on personal appearance and ability to communicate, as well as:

- Who knows whom?
- Who referred whom?
- Who is related to whom?
- Who owes whom a favor?
- Who wants to get in good with the person who made the referral?

The goal is to include all possible strategies and advantages in your job-search arsenal. You may be surprised by the number of people you know and how extensive your networks are when you tap into them. You are probably already networking without knowing it.

To expand your network, you should not hesitate to talk to everyone you know and everyone you meet, friends, family, your dry cleaner, people in restaurants, strangers on trains and planes, people where you worship, and anywhere else. Cast a wide net.

*John was employed by a mid-sized company as director of Staff Development. One Friday afternoon, his supervisor Hector, the vice president of Human Resources, simply walked into John's office and told him that the company they worked for had just lost two of its biggest clients. Projected cost-cutting measures included the elimination of John's division and the layoffs of John and the four people he supervised. John was out of a job.*

*Unfortunately, he had not seen it coming, so he was not prepared. Later that Friday evening, John and his girlfriend Ming went to dinner at the local pizza parlor, which was owned by the family of John's best friend, Troy. Troy, who was working that evening, came over to John and Ming's table to say hi and to ask John if he wanted to watch the football game together on Sunday.*

*With one look at John's face, Troy immediately realized that something was very wrong. He hesitated to intrude but was concerned, so he asked, "Hey, bro. Is everything okay? You look like someone died."*

*John, who was a proud young man, was not in the mood to share his bad news. Troy was his best friend, but John was embarrassed. Ming gave him a look and said, "You might as well tell him. He'll find out eventually."*

*When Troy heard that John had lost his job, he said, "I may know someone who can help." Lee Turner, one of the pizza parlor's frequent lunch customers, had been in that afternoon, and Troy had overheard him say to his colleague that he was looking for a training consultant. Troy tactfully connected Lee and John. The connection led to a temporary assignment for John, which turned into a permanent position at a slightly higher salary than John had made previously.*

You will be amazed that even strangers will be willing to help. So often, people—many of them women—go through life helping others but forget to ask for help for themselves. Never be afraid or too proud to ask for help. Tell people that you are looking for employment and what your skills and background are. Give or send them your résumé. If possible, meet them for coffee, dressed to send the message that they will not regret taking the time to meet with you.

Of course, remember that they are not obligated to you, and they have a choice. You want them to choose to help you and be glad—even proud—that they did.

*While waiting in the checkout line at the grocery store, Sela, a soft-spoken, mild-mannered young woman, overheard a conversation between a woman behind her named Molly and another woman in line.*

*Molly said that she conducted career-advice workshops for a local civic association. Sela waited for Molly outside the store, told her that she was looking for a job, and asked for her help.*

*After Sela described her efforts to find a job and her frustration—in her words, "No one will help me"—Molly agreed to review her résumé. She remembered that she had begun to offer the workshops to help people with their job searches.*

*Molly saw the problem right away: Sela's résumé did not showcase her skills. She had merely listed her work experience and described her responsibilities generically. There was no "oomph" in her descriptions of her extensive employment history.*

*For example, Sela said that she worked on a project with coworkers. After listening to her explanation of her role on the project, Molly changed it to "contributed substantially to the success of a departmental initiative that improved productivity by 20 percent." Employers love measurable results that demonstrate improvement.*

*Molly reworked the résumé, sent it to Sela, and awaited her response. It came as a pleasant surprise to Molly to learn that the changes she had made to Sela's résumé worked immediately.*

*Sela contacted Molly with great news: She had received a telephone interview! Again, she asked for Molly's help.*

*This time, Molly directed Sela to material on how to prepare for telephone and in-person interviews found on the www.youremploymentmatters.com website. Sela read the material, followed the recommendations, "practiced, practiced, and practiced," and landed a "live," in-person interview. She put on her interview outfit, sat in front of a mirror to see how she looked sitting down, and adjusted her outfit to achieve the look she desired.*

*Sela also practiced answering interview questions in front of her mirror. She nailed it! Sela told Molly that she had applied for an entry-level position but, because of her considerable experience, education, and interview performance, she was offered a higher position.*

*Although Sela attributed her success to Molly's contribution, Molly knew better. Sela was successful because she stepped outside her comfort zone and asked a stranger for help. As intelligent, educated, and otherwise talented as Sela is, she simply did not know how to position herself to achieve successful job-search results.*

## Preparation

**TIP 3-45 Adopt the Boy Scout motto—"Be Prepared"—by planning what you will say during a networking opportunity and practicing how you will say it.**

**First:** Prepare a 90-second marketing pitch that is a personal, self-serving commercial about YOU. It is an opportunity to highlight your attributes, such as verbal and written skills, technical skills, poise, presence, and personality. Your marketing pitch should include the following key points:

- Your experience, strengths, accomplishments
- The type of work or position you seek
- Why you are interested in that type of work or industry
- Why you are attending the event (optional)

You should allocate the 90 seconds as follows:

- A brief statement about your education (15 seconds)
- Your early work experience and key accomplishments (20 seconds)
- Your most recent experiences and key achievements (25 seconds)
- What you can do for an employer and what you have to offer, including soft skills and your future focus (30 seconds)

**Note:** Most of the time is devoted to what you can do for an employer. For many, if not most, a person's soft skills—such as problem solving and communication skills—and a positive attitude are as important to employers as education, employment experience, and technical proficiency.

Feel free to reallocate the 90 seconds for your work experience or education if it is particularly interesting or impressive. Keep in mind, however, that people value their time and may not be willing to listen to lengthy soliloquies. Make it short, interesting, and memorable, and deliver it crisply.

After a concise, informative marketing pitch is drafted, the next thing to do is practice, practice, practice. The objective is to achieve a smooth, polished delivery in 90 seconds that exudes confidence, competence, and professionalism.

**Make no mistake:** It takes time to draft and master an effective marketing pitch, but it is an invaluable tool that will be useful after you find employment.

*Christine, a former executive, attended a reception hosted by the alumni of a local university's business school. The well-attended event was held at a lovely venue with several large rooms and comfortable outside seating. It was an ideal networking opportunity.*

*Recent business school graduates Beth, Alexandra, and Jerry were introduced to attendees by professors or staff members. Each young person was poised, pleasant, and engaged. Everyone exchanged business cards.*

*After a discussion about the changes in the employment landscape and what young people needed to do to increase their employment opportunities, Christine said her goodbyes and left the reception to have dinner with friends in the main dining room.*

*Before she was seated, Jerry walked up to her with his hand extended and reintroduced himself. "Hello again, Ms. Bryant. I'm Jerry Charles. I met you inside at the reception. I just graduated with an MBA in marketing. I'm working at Global Company as an intern. I hope I'll get hired in a full-time position but, if I don't, I'm looking for a position with a company that can use my technical and marketing skills."*

*Christine was floored. It was as if Jerry had attended one of her career-readiness workshops. He understood that he had a limited amount of time to convey his message and pitch himself (as his product) persuasively and make a favorable impression. Jerry's marketing pitch was excellent!*

*Christine agreed to help Jerry with his efforts to find a job. When Jerry returned from vacation, she was not surprised to learn that her help was not needed. Jerry had been offered a position with a Fortune 500 company, which he accepted.*

You may notice that Jerry's pitch was short and did not cover his early work experience and key accomplishments. What Jerry delivered in a limited amount of time was impressive and compelling.

His professional appearance and demeanor, posture, and flawlessly delivered pitch sealed the deal for Christine. Jerry made her want to help him find a job.

**Second:** Mastering the social graces is another old-school approach that yields positive results. There is an opportunity to be viewed favorably during your job search by:

- Smiling
- Holding doors open
- Saying "please" and "thank you" to everyone who helps (even in a small way)
- Listening intently
- Making eye contact

If someone is especially kind or encouraging before or after an interview, find out the person's name and send the person a thank you note. Even better, try to find the individual after the interview to thank him or her in person. They will remember you favorably. If an employment opportunity arises, you may be the person they think of to assume the role because you left a positive impression.

An expression of your appreciation that you may consider an insignificant gesture and simply being polite may cause someone to conclude that you are the kind of person they want to work with each day.

Thank you notes should always be sent to contacts who have helped you and anyone who interviewed you individually or in a group. Your failure to do so may be considered a lack of interest or a glaring omission that will be held against you.

**Caution:** Do not assume that older individuals are not technically savvy. Many of them have wholeheartedly embraced new-school approaches to communication. Use your powers of observation and knowledge about the person to determine whether to use e-mail or snail mail to thank those with whom you have met or those who have helped you.

**Third:** Old-school familiarity with the rules of etiquette is also essential. Being aware of social etiquette enables you to make an informed decision about whether to follow the rules. Ignorance of the rules should never be an excuse for failing to make a good impression.

You do not want to give anyone the impression that you are not ready for prime time because you put your napkin under your chin at a business dinner or picked your teeth with your fingernail because that kernel of corn was driving you crazy. The purchase of Emily Post's *Etiquette*, 18th ed., in hardcover or paperback, which is a comprehensive, modern guide to managing yourself in polite society, may be in order. Alternatively, consider purchasing a series of books called Gentle Manners, which are easy-to-carry, quick references for social situations. Titles include:

- *How to Be a Gentleman Revised & Updated: A Contemporary Guide to Common Courtesy*[15]
- *How to Be a Lady Revised & Updated: A Contemporary Guide to Common Courtesy*[16]
- *As a Gentleman Would Say: Responses to Life's Important (and Sometimes Awkward) Situations*[17]
- *As a Lady Would Say Revised & Updated: Responses to Life's Important (and Sometimes Awkward) Situations*[18]

If your public library does not have them, ask the librarian to consider ordering them, or ask for any of them as a gift. Present yourself so there

[15] Bridges, J. 2012. *How to Be a Gentleman Revised & Updated: A Contemporary Guide to Common Courtesy (GentleManners)*. Nashville, TN: Rutledge Hill Press, https://amazon.com/s?k=how+to+be+a+gentlemen&i=stripbooks

[16] Simpson-Giles, C. 2012. *How to Be a Lady Revised & Updated: A Contemporary Guide to Common Courtesy (GentleManners)*. Nashville, TN: Thomas Nelson, https://amazon.com/s?k=how+to+be+lady+revised+and+expanded

[17] Bridges, J., and B. Curtis. 2012. *As a Gentleman Would Say: Responses to Life's Important (and Sometimes Awkward) Situations (GentleManners)*. Nashville, TN:Rutledge Hill Press, https://amazon.com/s?k=%E2%80%A2+As+a+Gentleman+Would+Say%3A+Responses

[18] Shade, S. 2012. *As a Lady Would Say Revised & Updated: Responses to Life's Important (and Sometimes Awkward) Situations (GentleManners)*. Nashville, TN: Thomas Nelson, https://amazon.com/s?k=%E2%80%A2+As+a+Lady+Would+Say%3A+Responses+to+Life

is no question that you are better suited than anyone else to represent the company as an employee.

Now you are ready for networking—old-school and new-school style: It may be difficult to believe, but there are so many ways people can help you, and they are usually willing. They simply may not think of how they can be helpful.

Make a list of the people you know and contact them all to tell them that you need a job. Tell them that you would like their help. It is up to you to identify how they can help.

Ask them if they can introduce you to other people who will introduce you to other people. Someone may be an HR person who can review your résumé and give you feedback.

Someone else may know someone else who has an open position. It is important to be specific about the type of position you seek.

Tell them you will call them to follow up and do so two weeks later if you have not heard from the person. Understand, however, that finding a job for you is higher on your "to-do" list than it is on the other person's list. It is important to give people time to contact others on your behalf.

Follow up persistently, but politely. You simply cannot afford to rely on anyone else to care as much about getting you employed as you do. Own your job search and manage it. If you sit back and wait for an e-mail or telephone call that may never come, you will likely be out of work for a long time.

Ask your contacts whether they have any advice for you, whether there is anyone they know who can give you a lead or give you advice, and to think about any possible opportunities no matter how indefinite. Be sure to write down everything and follow up.

Consider professional, community, and political events networking activities to attend where you meet people you know and people you do not know.

- Try to obtain the names of expected speakers and attendees in advance, so you can research them and connect with as many of them as possible.
- If you meet someone you admire or someone whose job you want to have one day, ask them lots of questions, such as:
  ○ "How did you achieve your goals?" (People love to talk about themselves.)

- "What challenges did you face along the way?"
- "What do you love about your job?"
- "What do you not like about your job?"

The mastery of your marketing pitch will help you engage people in conversation.

As you network, it is helpful to create a "win–win" situation by doing something that benefits the other person. For example, suppose one of your friends has an uncle who is an HR director at a company headquartered in the next town. You have a cousin who works for an advertising agency that represents the National Football League (NFL). Your cousin can get tickets to almost any NFL game, if the game is not sold out.

Before you make the offer to your friend, make sure your cousin can get the tickets. If your cousin cannot help you out, ask the friend to introduce you to the uncle anyway. Why not?

You have nothing to lose by identifying the people in your extended network and contacting them. Use your networks. Keep talking to people. They will tell you to call two friends and you will call them, and then they will tell you to call two more friends, and so on.

Looking for a job takes time and a lot of hard work for which there is no substitute. The possibilities are endless, but it takes time, patience, and perseverance.

First and foremost, people must know that you need and want help. To be sure that they know, tell them. Please do not leave it to anyone else. It is your future. Own it!

- Use and expand your networks by continuing to talk to people "live" and through social media.
- Do not let pride or ego get in the way.
- Take a deep breath and step outside your comfort zone.
- Introduce yourself to people you do not know and tell them that you are looking for work.
- Yes, you can talk to strangers. You are an adult on a mission.
- Do not succumb to fears and insecurities.
- If you do not think someone will be helpful, do not let that prevent you from connecting with the person. If nothing

else, you will have a new contact to add to your network database.

- The goal is to establish a vast network that will help you find a job.

**TIP 3-46 Maintain your network contacts and keep them updated.**
After securing employment, your network should be maintained. You will find it useful in the future. It is not unusual to lose data and contacts on smartphones, cell phones, and other electronic devices. It is inexcusable to miss an opportunity that could have led to a job because you failed to secure essential data.

As you network:

- Be sure to create a database.
- Back up the database on cloud storage and an external hard drive.
- All contacts (old and new), with names, e-mail, and home or business addresses and various telephone numbers, should be added to your electronic database and backed up.
- Let contacts hear from you even when you do not want anything.

**Do not get it twisted:** One more time—use social media but use it wisely. The new-school approach, which favors the speed of more impersonal electronic submissions and social networks to share information and communicate thoughts, ideas, hopes, and dreams, is a critical element of your networking strategy.

Unquestionably, tablets, laptops, smartphones, and various types of social media are useful tools and essential to achieving employment success. However, it is foolhardy to rely on them exclusively.

There was a time when people who wanted to work could find a job. As anyone who is currently looking for employment knows, times have changed. Nonetheless, the use of both old-school and new-school approaches to express yourself and your skills effectively and consistently as you persistently network is Your GPS to Employment Success.

**TIP 3-47 Master virtual networking.**

Admittedly, COVID-19 has impacted "live," in-person interactions, but virtual networking works remarkably well. In fact, it is a great alternative.

Businesses and organizations hold various meetings virtually. Thus, alumni, social and fraternal organizations, religious organizations, scholarship sources, and community-based entities are also possible sources of networking opportunities.

Training is conducted virtually. HR professionals in all industries, businesses, and organizations are probably all on LinkedIn. You must find them but complete your LinkedIn profile first.[19]

Begin by researching the employers you are interested in contacting. Go to their websites. Identify the names of senior leaders and contact them. Also, Google the business names. See what is written about them and who is mentioned. Contact whoever is mentioned.

That is a strategy, but before you proceed you must make sure that your marketing pitch is interesting, informative, and creates a "win–win." Consider filming a video of your marketing pitch.

Close with a "win–win." You must be creative to get your foot in the door. A version of the following: *If you hire me, you won't regret it. I'll arrive early. I'll pitch in where needed. I'll dot my "I"s and cross my "T"s. If permitted, I'll check to make sure you have the support you need for the day. If you don't, with your permission, I'll jump in to help.*

*If you give me a job, my job will be to make you look good and to make your job easier. I won't overpromise and underdeliver.*

Integrate your hard and soft skills in your "win–win" format. Do not include anything in your pitch that you are not willing to do.

Written materials like your cover letter should pique the reader's interest. Résumés should be two pages, devoid of typos, and include skills

---

19  Graham, J. 2020. "'You're Crazy If You're Not using LinkedIn': How to Master the Business Social Network." Blog, *USA Today,* June 12, 2020, https://usatoday.com/story/tech/2020/06/12/linkedin-tips-how-use-network-grow-businessfind-job/5338633002/

identified in the job description. These documents must be consistent with other relevant matter online or elsewhere.

A video of you delivering your marketing pitch is the substitute for your presence. Consequently, it must make viewers want to see and hear more. Hard and soft skills should be included in your materials.

Hard skills are learned abilities. For example,

- "Technical Skills. Skills that include specialized knowledge and expertise in fields such as IT....
- Computer Skills. Skills that include your abilities to use software and hardware....
- Analytical Skills. Skills that include gathering data, analyzing it....[and reporting it in a clear, concise format]
- Marketing Skills. Marketing skills that include the general knowledge of sales, advertising...."[20]

Soft skills are subjective or people skills including attributes like teamwork and collaboration, communication, work ethic, and accountability.[21]

Your video should be creative and interesting, yet professional, and your materials should reflect a knowledge of business trends such as artificial intelligence,[22] emotional intelligence, and robotics. For example, if you are interested in an HR job you should know the impact artificial intelligence and analytics have on hiring decisions.[23]

---

[20] Tomaszewski, M. 2020. "Hard Skills: Definition & List of Best Examples for Any Resume." *Blog, zety,* May 27, 2020, https://zety.com/blog/hard-skills

[21] Doyle, A. 2020. "Hard Skills vs. Soft Skills: What's the Difference?" Blog, *thebalancecareers,* updated January 20, 2020, https://thebalancecareers.com/hard-skills-vs-soft-skills-2063780

[22] Lotito, M.J., and M.U. Scherer. 2018. "Thought Leaders Predict AI's Impact on the Workforce." (Report of Roundtable of leaders from government, industry, and academia to discuss artificial intelligence, robotics, and other automation technologies hosted by the Littler Mendelson P.C. law firm), November 12, 2018, https://littler.com/files/wpi_thought_leaders_predict_ais_impact.pdf#:

[23] Schellmann, H. 2020. "How Job Interviews Will Transform in the Next Decade." January 7, 2020, (subscription required) https://wsj.com/articles/how-job-interviews-will-transform-in-the-next-decade-11578409136

Seasoned professionals recognize the value of networking generally and share the following suggestions/observations:

- Networking played a big role in the career of Julie Lane-Hailey, PhD.[24] She
  - Leveraged her connections, sought opportunities
  - Kept in touch with coworkers, friends, and peers
  - Cautions against discounting a short-term opportunity because she got a great job from an interview for a consulting gig
- James Huber, DMD,[25] advocates cultivating long-term relationships. He
  - Kept in touch with the people who awarded him scholarships to attend undergraduate and dental school
  - Maintained those relationships which led to opportunities well beyond scholarships
  - Also recommends connecting with leaders in the community and becoming an advocate for yourself and for others
- Based on his experience as a seasoned public employee, engineer Rodney Abrams[26]
  - Views networking as the best way to
    1. Aid in career growth
    2. Enhance and expand a person's exposures
    3. Crystallize career paths
    4. Get information critical to making professional, career, and personal life decisions

---

[24] Lane-Hailey, J. 2020. Your Employment Matter with Beverly Williams Podcast, "Who You Know Matters." https://youremploymentmatters.com/podcast/

[25] Huber, J. DMD. 2020. Your Employment Matter with Beverly Williams Podcast, "What is Your Destination and Do You Have a Plan?" https://your-employmentmatters.com/podcast/

[26] Ibid., Abrams, R. 2020. Your Employment Matter with Beverly Williams Podcast, "Learning to Rise in Your Career" https://youremploymentmatters.com/podcast/

- ○ Suggests
    1. Reading voraciously to learn and embrace new ideas
    2. That information acquired from reading coupled with robust networking can also make a person an interesting conversationalist
    3. Reading helps form mental models useful in problem solving and decision making
- ○ Recommends the following books:
    1. Stephen R. Covey, *The 7 Habits of Highly Effective People*
    2. Spencer Johnson, MD, *Who Moved My Cheese*
    3. David Allen, *Getting Things Done*

**Go forth and network!**

# CHAPTER 4

# Who Are You?

*Every decision you make—every decision—is not a decision about what to do. It's a decision about Who You Are.*

—Neale Donald Walsch,
American author, actor, screenwriter, and speaker

## Reflections

To be your authentic self, you will need to be honest about who you are and what you will and will not do. Are you satisfied with your personal brand or does it need work?

**TIP 4-48 Acknowledge perceptions about your strengths and weaknesses.**

**TIP 4-49 By your conduct, refute negative perceptions.**

Fairly or unfairly, some people draw conclusions and form judgments about others without firsthand knowledge or personal experience. If you were born between 1982 and 2000, you are a member of the generational cohort group, Generation Y, also known as Millennials. If you are also a recent college graduate with little or no experience, the favorable perceptions about you are that you:

- Begin with a clean slate, and you can be trained, developed, and molded into the type of employee an employer wants
- May be eager to take any job, especially one that promises advancement

- Have a "sixth sense" that enables you to incorporate technology into your personal and global interactions
- Are family centric
- Are achievement and team oriented[1]

Less favorable perceptions include the idea that you lack experience, which means that you need to be trained. Training takes time and resources. Typically, employers prefer someone who can hit the ground running and function with minimal supervision.

Additionally, less favorable perceptions are that:

- You may be used to hand-holding and one-on-one attention.
- You may not respect authority.
- You may have unrealistic expectations about your potential.
- You may not accept the concept of teamwork.
- You are not prepared for work/life realities.
- You lack focus.

Perceptions depend on the person who has them, their personal experience with and exposure to members of the group, and the last person to whom they spoke. Unfortunately, sometimes perception is reality. If none of these traits apply to you, nonetheless, be aware of them.

**Do not get it twisted:** Dispel negative perceptions while conveying that you are a hard worker, a fast learner, willing to take on any job, and the person who should be hired or promoted.

*Begin somewhere; you cannot build a reputation on what you intend to do.*

—Liz Smith,
American gossip columnist and journalist (1923 to 2017)

---

[1] Kane, S. 2019. "The Common Characteristics of Millennial Professionals, Blog." *thebalancecareers,* Updated May 28, 2019. https://thebalancecareers .com/common-characteristics-of-generation-y-professionals-2164683; Deloitte & Touche; Generation Y Changing with the times; 2011 https://www2.deloitte. com/content/dam/Deloitte/ie/Documents/People/Generation_Y.pdf

**Your personal brand:** Personal branding is a concept that increasingly more people recognize as an essential element in managing careers and an individual's personal marketing. Examples of attributes which may create a personal brand include:

- Verbal and written communication skills
- Technical knowledge
- Personal appearance
- Social media use[2]
- Attitude
- Integrity
- Work ethic

Also consider the following definition, "[y]our personal brand is what people say about you when you're not in the room."[3] If you type an e-mail or have a conversation with a friend or family member, you are branding yourself. How you dress casually, professionally, and for more formal occasions contributes to your brand.

How you dress, what you eat, and how you talk all contribute to your brand. Think of your brand as the summation of all the associations about you stored in people's minds.[4]

---

[2] Pavlina, S. 2019. "Personal Branding." Blog, *Steve Pavlina,* December 20, 2019, http://stevepavlina.com/blog/2008/02/

[3] *BestMeBrand,* Blog, "Personal Branding: What Do You Want People to Say About You?" May 2, 2018, quoting Jeffrey P. Bezos, Chief Executive Officer, Amazon, https://bestmebrand.com/blog/what-is-personal-branding/

[4] See, "Personal Brand Workbook." *PricewaterhouseCoopers;* https://pwc.com/c1/en/assets/downloads/personal_brand_workbook.pdf

To summarize, your personal brand is:

- How you present yourself to others
- Your reputation
- How people describe you
- What people think of you

Consider how people who know you will describe you. At minimum, the elements identified should form the foundation for your personal brand. Seemingly insignificant elements of your individual style and preferences may also contribute to your personal brand.

It is important to be able to articulate how you describe yourself and what you think of yourself.

*Several college friends attended a personal branding workshop. Each person was asked to complete a five-item questionnaire.*

*One of the questions was "Do you know how people describe you? If you don't know, how do you describe yourself?"*

*Bailey completed the short questionnaire in record time and volunteered to share her responses with the others. She said that people think she is funny and so does she.*

*The workshop leader asked Bailey if she would respond differently during a job interview. She said, "no."*

Bailey's answer was not inappropriate. A better answer is, I have a good sense of humor. Clowns are funny. The objective is to give an answer that does not cause you to be considered as other than mature and professional.

As the following story conveys, you may be observed and conclusions drawn about you merely because of what you bring with you to a meeting.

*Nick, a young manager with executive aspirations, attended many meetings with company executives. It never occurred to him that anyone was paying attention to him during most of these meetings because he was usually along to crunch numbers and provide information to Mahish, his boss, who was a senior vice president.*

*After one meeting, Rebecca, another senior vice president, stopped Nick and said, "I've noticed that you always have a little notebook with you. They're attractive notebooks with different patterns."*

*Nick was surprised, but kept his cool, and replied, "I like a nice notebook, something more than the typical spiral notebook."*

*Rebecca smiled and responded, "I also like a nice notebook, and so does my husband. Where do you buy yours?"*

Thereafter, Nick was on Rebecca's radar screen, which was not a bad place to be. Who would have thought that a notebook would contribute to Nick's effort to distinguish himself at work? What skills do you think the notebook conveyed?

## Reputation

*The way to gain a good reputation is to endeavor to be what you desire to appear.*

—Socrates (ancient Greek philosopher, 470 BC to 399 BC)

*A reputation once broken may possibly be repaired, but the world will always keep their eyes on the spot where the crack was.*

—Joseph Hall,
English bishop, moral philosopher, and satirist (1574 to 1656)

**TIP 4-50 Strive to establish a reputation as a person who is hard working, detail oriented, honest, ethical, reliable, punctual, polite, and a team player.**

**TIP 4-51 View yourself as a professional.**

**TIP 4-52 By your conduct, create that impression so that others view you likewise.**

If you are just starting out, and you do not have a reputation that precedes you, establish one you can be proud of by conducting yourself with integrity and maturity. Additionally, whatever your career ambitions are, it is imperative that you are viewed as a professional. Your conduct should reinforce that perception.

Your public and private behavior, including what you say, how you say it, and how you present yourself, influence how you are perceived by others. Your reputation evolves over time based on these perceptions and the opinions that result from them.

- A good reputation takes a long time to build and only moments to destroy.
- Rehabilitating your reputation is possible, but it also takes a strategic plan and time to execute the plan.
- A leopard can change its spots, but it takes time and positive experiences to convince skeptics.
- If your reputation needs improvement, change it.
  1. Be prepared to talk about the changes you have made.
  2. Explain why you have changed.
  3. By your conduct, demonstrate that you are no longer the person you once were.

In the workplace, your reputation may precede you. If it does, you always want it said that you are a reliable, hard worker, who is creative and resourceful (in other words, someone who thinks outside the box) as well as a person of good character and integrity, who can be relied upon to tell the truth.

Do workers who are dishonest and unfamiliar with the truth prosper? Unfortunately, some of them do, but do not try it. It is not worth the risk.

Before you begin to market yourself in interviews and as you network, find out how self-aware you are by asking:

- "Who am I?"
- "What is my personal brand?"
- "Does my personal brand serve me well or do I need to make changes?"

*Mario, a young contestant on a popular talent show, demonstrated a sense of self-awareness that is rare, even in older adults. In his interview, which aired as part of the show, Mario said he was in the competition because he needed to know whether he was a talented singer.*

*His parents consistently told Mario how well he sang, but he realized that his parents are biased because they love him. Mario wanted independent, objective affirmation that he had the talent his parents always told him he had.*

*Unfortunately, Mario did not win his round, but he won my respect and admiration because he dared to do what many people never even think of.*

*It would have been easier for Mario to believe the positive feedback from his parents and to believe what he wanted to be true, but Mario courageously sought information, not affirmation. (See Tip 1-23.)*

Like Mario, you need information that will help you be successful rather than affirmation that you are as wonderful as you have been led to believe. As mentioned earlier, ask people who know you and whom you respect such as teachers, coaches, and clergy, what your strengths and weaknesses are.

You need to find out whether you are:

- An effective communicator
- A team player
- Reliable
- A leader or a person with leadership qualities or a person with special attributes (If you are, ask them to please list them for you.)

Do not forget to accept feedback as you would a gift: gratefully and graciously. (See Tip 1-18.) Ask people if they want their feedback to be anonymous. If they do, give them a self-addressed, stamped envelope, and ask that they mail their response to you. If they do not require anonymity, they can e-mail their response.

Be sure to send them a written thank you note. How a thank you is sent depends on what you know about the person. If you know the person is more traditional and may prefer a handwritten note via snail mail, do not send an e-mail. An e-card or e-mail that expresses your appreciation for his or her time and feedback is acceptable, if you are sure that the person will not consider it too casual.

*We are all different and should do what we can do to remain so.*
—Paulo Coelho, lyricist and novelist

**TIP 4-53 Embrace differences.**

**TIP 4-54 Learn from people who are different.**

**TIP 4-55 Overcome prejudice and biases.**

Different is not wrong or inferior; it is simply different. If you go through life avoiding everyone who is not the same as you, you will miss out on a large slice of life and some great experiences.

Regardless of your age or stage in life, you are subject to the vagaries of the inner workings of the employment environment. Consequently, you will be interacting with others who will be different from you, have different beliefs, and have different ways of doing things.

Each generation is influenced by its own defining events and technologies and has something to offer the team effort. It is counterproductive and rude to be impolite or to summarily dismiss someone's ideas simply because they are different or unfamiliar to you.

Currently, there are five different generations employed in the workplace:

- Mature/World War II generation (born before 1946)
- Baby Boomer generation (born between 1946 and 1964)
- Generation X (born between 1965 and 1980)
- Generation Y/Millennials (born 1981 to 1996)
- Generation Z (born after 1997)[5]

If you have a degree, do not mentally dismiss the contributions of individuals who may not have degrees. Acknowledge the importance of their industry and life experience and institutional knowledge.

**Learn:** One of the benefits of working in a multigenerational environment is that there are so many opportunities to learn something new because everyone brings something unique to the discussion. Men and women of different ages, ethnicities, national origins, and religions, regardless of their sexual and gender expressions, and/or disabilities and abilities, all have something to contribute.

Consider your coworkers and their differences as an instructional opportunity. You will be exposed to a variety of cultures, different ways of

---

[5] Dimock, M. 2019. "Defining Generations: Where Millennials end and Generation Z begins." Blog *Fact Tank,* Pew Research Center, January 17, 2019, https://pewresearch.org/fact-tank/2019/01/17/where-millennials-end-and-generationz-begins/

doing things, and points of view. Your coworkers may be your senior in years of service and work experience. A working environment can present content-rich networking and learning opportunities. Do not overlook these times to acquire knowledge and information free of charge.

If you are employed, workplace interactions with people who are different include:

- Taking their direction and supervision
- Accepting their solicited and unsolicited feedback, which may be favorable or unfavorable
- Interacting with coworkers, clients, customers, and other third parties who do not even work for your employer

If you are unemployed, interactions include:

- Following directions
- Answering questions
- Waiting for interviews to begin
- Waiting for decisions to be made and for you to be notified of them

Keep in mind that people who do not look or sound like you are people who may make decisions about your employment matters. These decision makers are looking for people who will contribute to a team and with whom they and other employees want to work with each workday.

Make every effort to disregard pre-existing biases and prejudices.

**TIP 4-56 Do not let your ego get in the way. If you do not know, say so.** Regardless of where you are in your career, you are not likely to know how to do everything you will be asked to do or be able to answer every question you are asked. If you are looking for employment, you should anticipate questions that might be asked as you network and interview and practice your responses.

If you are employed, anticipate questions that might come up in the discussion or presentation, and be prepared with answers and information. If the questions do not come up and you think the material you have is relevant and helpful, include the information in a question.

You might ask:

- "Have we looked at the impact that weather may have on deliveries?"
- "Do we need to consider whether different time zones make any difference?"
- "Have we considered local customs and practices?"

Then explain why the information you have is relevant to the discussion.

If you do not have all the answers (and you will not), do not let your ego get in the way. There is no shame in admitting that you do not know. You may be ashamed and embarrassed if "you attempt to perpetrate a fraud" and get caught. Decide whether to admit that you do not know, or make every effort to find the answer, and then admit that you do not know.

If time is a critical factor, consider immediately confessing your limitations. Declare that you will make every effort to find the answer, and provide an update within a reasonable, realistic period. Then exhaust your contacts and resources to gather the information you need.

Whether or not you have it, you must provide an update as promised. Circumstances will dictate whether you will be given more time to come up with the information and perhaps someone to assist you.

## Personal Appearance

*Clothes and manners do not make the man [or woman]; but, when he [or she] is made, they greatly improve his [or her] appearance.*

—Henry Ward Beecher
(U.S. Congregational minister, 1813 to 1887)

**TIP 4-57 Your personal appearance can help you get hired or cause you to be disregarded.**

**TIP 4-58 Your clothes should not enter the room before you do because you are more important than your clothes.**

**TIP 4-59 Before you leave for work or for an interview, look in the mirror and ask yourself, "Is this the statement I want to make?"**

**TIP 4-60 Do not be fooled by workplace dress codes that permit "business casual" or "dress-down" days.**

**TIP 4-61 Emulate the style of dress that is common at the level of the position you aspire to achieve.**

When creating or modifying your personal brand, consider that:

- Personal appearance is critically important.
- You only have one opportunity to make a first impression. (It is trite and a cliché, but it is true.)
- Before you utter a word, you will be sized up and judged correctly or incorrectly as to whether or not you are suitable for a position or promotional opportunity.

*The Muppets are dearly loved, but Miss Piggy is an icon. She is known to be a fashionista and a diva, and intolerant of anyone who tries to treat her as other than the star she presumes to be.*

*For whatever reason, Miss Piggy dropped out of sight for a few years. She was missed. Miss Piggy roared back into the high-profile media limelight to promote a movie..*

*Though absent or maintaining a low profile for a time, she kept her brand intact and unchanged. Her glorious, high-profile return considerably enhanced and elevated her personal brand. Miss Piggy's crowning achievement was being the subject of a feature article in an issue of InStyle fashion magazine. Miss Piggy is indeed The Notorious P.I.G!*

Presenting the appropriate appearance as you search for a job or compete for a promotional opportunity is essential. Your attire should send a silent but emphatic message that you are the person to hire or promote.

**What is appropriate?** Appropriateness depends on the industry, business culture, geographic location of the business, and the position itself. It also depends on the people who make decisions about who will be hired or promoted.

- If your preference is to dress like an entertainer, and you are applying for a job as a teacher or a lawyer, or for a position in a conservative Fortune 500 company, leave the stage clothes at home. Entertainers rarely dress in a manner appropriate for traditional workplaces.

- If you are dissatisfied with your appearance and have been planning to address it sometime in the future, the future is now.

At the very least, keep in mind that:

- Whatever is worn must fit well and be neat, clean, and pressed.
- Trousers must be worn up on the waist and with a belt if there are belt loops.
- Socks must be worn, sneakers must not be worn, and shoes must be shined.
- Depending on the industry, open-toe shoes and sandals may be inappropriate.
- Personal hygiene must never detract from your otherwise appropriate appearance.
- Using too much perfume, cologne, or aftershave in the workplace can be problematic for people with allergies or sensitivity to smells or odors.
- Tattoos and body piercings should be covered (depends on the job sought and the industry).
- Vibrant, quirky hair colors, braids, dreadlocks (unless you are competing on American Idol or Hell's Kitchen), mohawks, and spiky hair may raise an eyebrow. As with other forms of discrimination, there are laws against hair discrimination. You may have to make a choice.

In other words, before you open your mouth, your appearance speaks for you. You may want to observe employees leaving the place where you are applying to check out what they are wearing.

Consider these examples:

*As an assistant dean, James has consistently lobbied the university that employs him to provide more career-readiness support for its students. An important meeting scheduled for the next day was, in James's opinion, the best opportunity to achieve his goal. University administrators and several faculty members were expected to attend.*

*He needed visual support for his position because it was clear to him that his speeches and discussions were not persuasive enough to convince the dean to allocate additional funds to the career-counseling department. James did not know what he was looking for, but he knew that he would recognize it when he saw it, and he did.*

*After surfing the Internet for what seemed like hours, James saw the picture that conveyed his message better than any words he had chosen thus far. It was a picture of the university's students at a job fair that had taken place the previous year. The men and women were appropriately dressed and otherwise well groomed, but there was something missing.*

*James made copies of the picture and distributed them at the meeting the next day. Those in attendance listened to James as he implored them to support his cause and allocate more money for career readiness.*

*The dean commented that, based on the picture and the report she had received, the job fair was very well attended by corporations and other businesses looking for talent and students looking for jobs.*

*James agreed, but then asked her and the other attendees to look closely at the picture and ask themselves, "Which of the students in the picture made them reach for their wallets to hire them?"*

*What surprised everyone in the room was that the camera had captured the lack of energy of the students in the picture. It was obvious from one student's stooped shoulders and bent head that he was not emitting a "hire me" image. Another student was yawning with his mouth wide open. One woman appeared bored with the entire process.*

*Quite simply, there was no energy from the students; instead, they appeared disengaged, distracted, and uninterested. Admittedly, it was one frame—a snapshot on a day when there were many more—but, as James emphasized, the students in the picture had missed an opportunity to stand out among other attendees.*

*He also reminded the dean that, of the approximately one hundred undergraduates and graduates who had attended the job fair, only four received interviews, and not one had received a job offer.*

*Michelle is a young woman who was hired to supervise an HR team at a New York City company. She arrived for her first day of work dressed professionally and appropriately in a lovely pantsuit and pumps, with what she considered just the right amount of jewelry.*

*According to Michelle, "I wore my wedding rings, a silver watch, small silver ball earrings, and a silver necklace." Shortly after Michelle arrived on her first day, Steve, her new boss, asked to speak to her. Appearing somewhat uncomfortable, Steve said, "Michelle, our company is very conservative. I hope I do not offend you, but would you consider not wearing the tiny gold hoop pierced earrings?"*

*Michelle "got it" and immediately put Steve at ease by telling him not to worry because she would gladly remove them. For years, she had worn the tiny hoops in the upper portion of her ears in addition to the larger earrings she wore in her earlobes. To her credit, Michelle recognized that removing the tiny hoops was in her long-term best interest.*

Decide on the message you want your appearance to convey and deliver that message. A word of caution to men and women: "To thine own self be true."

- Do not dress to convey a message you are not prepared to live with once you get the job. If you must express your individuality, wear brightly colored or provocative undergarments. You will know it is there, and a prospective employer should not have a clue.
- Thong underwear that can be seen is a bad idea for work wear. A thong revealed also sends a message that draws attention away from your stellar work performance and toward your physical attributes.
- If you are a trend-setting fashionista, interviews with traditional, conservative companies are not the venue for asserting your "cutting-edge fashion sense."

Take care not to give the impression that you are frivolous because of the trendy clothes you wear and the time you spend focusing on your clothing. You will appear frivolous if:

- You cannot walk to the copier because your feet hurt in five-inch heels.
- You are irritable because your clothes are too tight and uncomfortable.

- You are walking around the office too much because you want everyone to see your clothing.
- You do not like the people you work with because they do not wear "fab" outfits like you.

You may be a fantastic worker, but you are headed in the wrong direction if your clothing speaks louder than your talent. There should never be a perception that you are focusing on your clothing too much.

Do not be fooled because no one speaks negatively about your fashion statement. It is difficult to criticize someone's dress unless it violates the employer's dress code or is considered offensive.

So, what do employers do? At the very least, they do not hire someone whose style of dress is something they consider inappropriate or a distraction. They also might marginalize employees who do not present a suitable image.

*Gina, a recent college graduate, interviewed with a brokerage firm for an entry-level administrative position. She wore a dark suit and pumps to the interview; her hairstyle was as conservative as her outfit.*

*Gina was hired and performed her duties so well that she was given increasingly more responsibility. Unfortunately, Gina felt constrained by her conservative clothing and decided, "I have to be me."*

*She adopted a funky hairstyle appropriate for a more liberal working environment. Gina also began to dress in vibrant, two-piece outfits with flowing fabric and floral prints. She was surprised when she no longer received more responsibility and was not promoted.*

*Many years later, Gina told this story to another woman who asked her why she did not just wear brightly colored underwear. Gina responded, "I was young at the time and did not know better." She does not know for sure that her new image prevented her from moving forward, but she believes that was the problem because the brokerage firm was very conservative.*

### Females

If you want to be taken seriously, save form-fitting, tight clothing for nonwork-related occasions.

- Wear the proper undergarments that suppress jiggles and bounces, and make sure the "girls" are adequately covered and supported.
- The length of your skirt or dress should be long and loose enough that it will be unnecessary to tug at the hem to cover your thighs.
- If you are comfortable in the clothes you wear, it is one less thing to worry about.
- If you want to wear a new outfit, try everything on at least two days before you plan to wear it to make sure that you will look the way you envisioned.
- If you do not take these precautions regarding your clothing, your appearance may detract from your interview or job performance.
- Some major department and cosmetic stores offer free makeup makeovers with the purchase of products.

### Males

- Depending on the type of job you are looking for or the culture of the company you are employed by, facial hair may be a problem. More conservative companies frown upon beards and mustaches, especially on their client-facing executives and future executives.
- If you are applying for a position that is not a corporate role:
  - A white shirt and dark necktie with dark or khaki slacks may be worn with a sport jacket, if you have one.
  - A sweater in a neutral color will work if you do not have or cannot afford a sport coat.
  - If your career plans include rising through the management hierarchy of a conservative Fortune 500 company, mirroring the general appearance of the company's executives and current high-potential employees (to the extent you can identify them) is advisable. For example, you can wear a navy suit, an innocuous necktie, and a crisp white shirt.
  - You may want to drive by the place to check out male employees going in and out of the company parking lot.

Whatever you decide, a neat, well-groomed appearance is your objective. You should be aware that managers, as previously mentioned, may have personal biases about many things, including what clothing is appropriate to wear to work. They may not view your choice of clothing as appropriate for those who should rise in the organization.

This viewpoint may not be expressed, but it can be one of many considerations that affect you. If you have limited resources, shop for your employment wardrobe judiciously. Consignment shops in affluent communities have work appropriate formerly expensive clothing.

Clothing that looks the same can cost hundreds, even thousands of dollars more or less. For example, a white shirt or blouse purchased for $25 may look the same as a shirt or blouse that cost $100. The price tag will alert you that there is a difference, probably a huge one. The quality of the fabric, stitching, and tailoring of the more expensive garment should be superior to the similar garment that costs considerably less.

However, for employment-related purposes, the less expensive garment is adequate if it is properly cared for, which includes hanging it up after each use and laundering and ironing it as needed. The objective is to present an image that causes the interviewer or your supervisor to think of you first to fill an open position.

Regardless of gender or gender expression, dress according to these guidelines:

- Clean, crisp shirts and blouses
- Well-pressed dark suits, slacks, and jackets
- Pantyhose or tights and dark dress socks (long enough to reach almost to the knee)
- A few pieces of understated jewelry for women; a watch and a ring for men

To ensure that you make the appropriate choice of attire, you should ask a knowledgeable person or have a friend call HR, and then ask a young person whose fashion sense you admire how to make your look just a little trendy.

Also, research and analyze the appearance of on-air media personalities that most closely reflect the fashion statement you want to make. It is important to ensure that your fashion statement aligns with the company or business culture where you want to work.

Perhaps it is a belt, handbag, tie, or pocket square that provides that needed pop of color. If it is an ultra-traditional employer, an unseen pop of color that only you know about will be your secret.

Bottom line: You want to look good, be comfortable, and be dressed appropriately. A hardworking, committed employee will be working long hours. Uncomfortable, trendy clothing can make an eight-hour workday seem like 20 hours.

### TIP 4-62 Do not forget to master the social graces.

Remember that the workplace is a microcosm of society and the world. Unfortunately, the negative aspects of some people's personalities and behavior, such as rudeness, crudeness, or a lack of civility, can be characteristic of individuals employed at all levels in the workplace. Common courtesy, which includes civility and politeness, should be mandatory behavior, but it is not.

**Business events:** Company-sponsored events attended by employees and guests who are not employed by the host company offer another opportunity to distinguish yourself, whether you are looking for a job or are already hired. Even if you think you hold your liquor well, do not make the mistake of drinking to the point that you relax in demeanor or speech.

Drinking club soda with a twist gives the impression that you are drinking, but allows you to keep your wits about you. Many foolish incidents occur at business social events where alcohol is served. Drink when you get home. You do not want any part of the drama.

When you attend a networking or work-sponsored event, or represent your company, you must always be on your best behavior.

**Table (dining) etiquette:** At networking or work-related events, or occasions where coworkers are in attendance, good table manners are mandatory. Do not reach across the table for anything. Instead, ask the nearest person to pass it to you. Place your napkin in your lap, not under your chin.[6]

---

[6] Diamond, L. n.d. 13 *Little Etiquette Rules to Follow When You're Dining at a Restaurant,* Reader's Digest, March 21, 2020, https://rd.com/list/dining-etiquette/

Eat slowly and focus on the conversation. You will be surprised by what you learn as well as your ability to contribute to the conversation to your advantage. It is better to leave hungry, well informed, having put your "best foot forward" than to have had the spaghetti and meatballs or lobster.

**TIP 4-63 Always treat people the way you want to be treated and require the same from others.**

**TIP 4-64 Be courteous, pleasant, and helpful to everyone, including administrative assistants and other support staff.**

People should treat others the way they want to be treated themselves. This familiar rule governs or should govern interpersonal exchanges regardless of position or station in life. Sadly, it does not. If your supervisor hears positive, complimentary comments about your performance from support staff, this can only work in your favor.

**TIP 4-65 Whether you are looking for a job or already have one, do not make the mistake of being rude and disrespectful to administrative and support staff.**

Intuitively, you may know that you must bring your "A" game and "manage up" whenever you interact with executives. "Managing down" should also be a no-brainer but, for many individuals, it is not even a consideration. If you think that you do not need to be polite and civil to administrative, cafeteria, maintenance, and other support staff, perhaps you should reconsider.

You may not realize it, but support personnel are the eyes and ears of the workplace. Executives may speak freely in front of them because they are trusted or long-term employees, or because the executives are simply unaware of their presence.

Moreover, administrative assistants can be extremely helpful to job applicants and employees at every level if they choose to be helpful. For instance, if you have a rush job, your assistant is more likely to stay longer and help a considerate person than a rude one. It is in your best interest for them to like you because, without your knowledge and because of an actual or perceived slight, these same employees can become formidable enemies.

Your goal should be to establish relationships and contacts that are mutually beneficial. You do not want anyone, subtly or overtly, to fail to take that extra small step to provide you with information or otherwise do a favor for you, if they are free to do so. If you are nice to people, most people will be nice to you.

**Personality:** After you review the list below, decide which type of person you would prefer to work with each day.

1. Adventurous: someone who is outgoing and not afraid to try new things
2. Friendly: someone who is easy to get along with
3. Helpful: someone who likes to assist others
4. Honest: someone who is truthful
5. Capable: someone who is able to achieve things
6. Dishonest: someone who is not truthful
7. Impatient: someone who does not display patience
8. Childish: someone who behaves immaturely
9. Insecure: someone who lacks confidence
10. Selfish: someone who puts himself or herself before others[7]

If you are honest, you will admit that the first five traits listed are preferable to the second five traits. While most people do not have all of the previously listed personality traits, many have a mixture of those traits.

Completely overhauling your personality is unrealistic but making adjustments may be absolutely necessary to be successful in employment matters. Quite simply, you must stand out for the right reasons. Distinguish yourself from the many, many job applicants and promotion seekers by exuding skill, maturity, poise, and professionalism.

---

[7] Davenport, B. 2015. "List Of 600 Personality Traits." February 15, 2015 https://liveboldandbloom.com/02/self-awareness/list-of-personality-traits#6-list-of-600-personality-traits

**Do not misunderstand**: If you are in your 20s, you are not expected to project the maturity and presence of a 50-year-old, experienced businessperson. If you need to make a change, it will take work, practice, and focus, but you can do it because failure is not an option. There may be setbacks, perhaps more than you expected, but do not accept failure as a permanent outcome.

### TIP 4-66 Fine tune your communication skills.

Conveying thoughts, information, and opinions in writing and orally is a critical skill in workplace environments. Based on feedback you have received throughout your life, by now you should know whether you have strong communication skills.

If you do not write well, you should make an effort to improve. You never know when you may be asked to write a report, a service order, or a memorandum. Why not contact the adult education program in your community and enroll in a business writing course? It is better to have and not need than to need and not have.

A public-speaking course or organization such as Toastmasters[8] will also help you develop skills that will benefit you. Good public-speaking skills are important if you want to achieve success in connection with employment matters and community and political arenas.

Toastmasters is a nonprofit educational organization that teaches not only public speaking but leadership skills through a worldwide network of clubs. Public speaking exercises build self-confidence and provide practice writing speeches and giving presentations.[9] There are more than 1,680 clubs in 143 countries. The dues are U.S. $45 every six months, plus a new member fee of $20.[10]

All means of communication you use for employment-related matters must convey that you are a mature, professional adult. Hopefully, you now realize that your e-mail address and the greeting on your cell phone should not be provocative, playful, or immature, and you understand why.

---

[8] Toastmasters International http://toastmasters.org/
[9] Ibid.
[10] Ibid.

If you have not acquired a suitable e-mail address and recorded a more mature greeting on any phone on which you expect to receive a business call, please take care of these things:

- Keep your e-mail address and greeting simple.
- Identify yourself by using your first and last name in your e-mail address and greeting. Smile when you record your greeting, so it comes through in the recording.
- Speak clearly and stand up when you record the greeting.

Here are some areas of communication and the etiquette associated with each type:

**E-mail**

- Do not draft and send an e-mail when you have been drinking or under the influence of medication or drugs that cause drowsiness or euphoria or impairs your thinking. No matter how well you think you are functioning, it is not a wise move.
- Individuals you contact by e-mail should receive the same (or better) quality of interaction you give individuals on the telephone or face to face.
- Use the "high-importance" icon for time-sensitive messages.
- Do not use all lowercase or all uppercase letters.
- Write your message as you would say it if the person were in front of you.
- Use the rules of punctuation and grammar; do not rely on program features, including spell check.
- The subject line should accurately convey the topic addressed in the message.
- Include a space between paragraphs to make the message easier to read.
- Read the entire message out loud before you press the "send" button.

There are more rules at *How to Mind Your Manners With Email Etiquette.*[11]

**TIP 4-67 Practice cell phone and texting etiquette. Remember every phone call is not an emergency.**

- Cell phone and texting
  - Use electronic devices, such as your cell phone or smartphone, considerately.
  - Use your cell phone only for important calls.
  - Do not use your cell phone in the restroom because of background noises and the lack of privacy.
  - Do not bring your cell phone to meetings.
  - Only text on your time (e.g., lunch hours or breaks).
- During interviews, at work, and during work-related events:
  - Turn off your cell phone or set it on vibrate.
  - Let your cell phone calls go to voice mail during interviews and set it on vibrate during office hours.
  - Find a private place to make cell phone calls.

Furthermore, if you are looking for a job, you should always regularly check for messages left on your cell phone and return them immediately. The message may lead to an interview, which may lead to a job.

It is not enough to check the phone numbers of incoming calls on caller ID. You need to know what the person said in the message left for you. Additional information may be needed, an interview may be rescheduled, or there may be some other important reason that you need to retrieve your messages. Remember to return phone calls as soon as possible after you retrieve the message.

Once you begin your job search and after you are hired, always answer your cell phone, even after work hours. It could be a prospective employer

---

[11] Tschabitscher, H. 2020. "How to Mind Your Manners With Email Etiquette." Blog, Updated on May 01, 2020, https://lifewire.com/fundamental-email-etiquette-1171187

who wants to schedule an interview, or your boss with an assignment that can get you the promotion you want.

**Telephone**

Each time you answer the telephone:

- Smile. It will keep you positive and upbeat.
- Identify yourself; if appropriate, identify the business.
- Sound professional.
- Be pleasant.
- Be helpful.

Do not check your voicemail messages on speaker phone because you never know what your friends have said or the language they may have used.

### *Greeting (Avoid Handshakes) Guidelines*

Thanks to COVID-19, handshakes are now avoided. Greetings and goodbyes are determined by mutual agreement. Perhaps bowing, bumping elbows or feet will do. Whatever you do,

- Smile, and look directly into the person's eyes unless maintaining eye contact is not a common practice in your culture.
- Introduce yourself at a company event or an industry conference.
  - They will remember that you initiated your gesture first.
  - The gesture suggests two positive traits: confidence and maturity.

Your brand is the story you project and, by your conduct, reinforce. Who you are depends on who you want and commit to be. The common theme is that you are the driving force. Once you establish your personal brand and are satisfied that it conveys the message and image you desire, you should protect it.

Do not permit your brand to be diluted by engaging in behavior that diminishes your reputation. It is also possible for others close to you to adversely impact your brand, or at least cause people to raise an eyebrow to question conduct because of your association with them.

It is up to you to preserve the integrity of your brand. Any successful businessperson will confirm that this is true.

## Resources

- "Personal Brand Workbook." PricewaterhouseCoopers https://pwc.com/c1/en/assets/downloads/personal_brand_workbook.pdf
- John Bridges, How to Be a Gentleman Revised & Updated: A Contemporary Guide to Common Courtesy (GentleManners), Nashville, TN: Rutledge Hill Press (2012)
- Candace Simpson-Giles, How to Be a Lady Revised & Updated: A Contemporary Guide to Common Courtesy (GentleManners), Nashville, TN: Thomas Nelson (2012)
- John Bridges and Bryan Curtis, As a Gentleman Would Say: Responses to Life's Important (and Sometimes Awkward) Situations (GentleManners), Nashville, TN: Rutledge Hill Press (2012)
- Sheryl Shade, As a Lady Would Say Revised & Updated: Responses to Life's Important (and Sometimes Awkward) Situations (GentleManners), Nashville, TN: Thomas Nelson (2012)

# CHAPTER 5

# What Do You Bring to the Table?
# What Is Your Destination?

*You've got to be careful if you don't know where you're going, 'cause you might not get there.*

—Yogi Berra, former American Major League
Baseball catcher, outfielder, and manager

*If you are clear about what you want, the world responds with clarity.*

—Loretta Staples, a graphic, exhibit and interaction designer

**TIP 5-68 Conduct a self-assessment.**

Now that you are out of school or ready to change careers, what do you want to be? Whether you have just graduated, are ready to choose a different career, or simply find yourself unexpectedly unemployed, it is helpful to conduct a self-assessment and develop a career plan for several reasons. Four of the most important reasons are that:

- You will acquire a heightened awareness of your talents, strengths, and weaknesses.
- The information you acquire will make it easier to draft your marketing pitch, résumés, and cover letters.
- It gives you the opportunity to think about what factors are important to you in an employment context.
- It may also keep you focused.

There are articles that will help you gather information and gain insight about yourself. For example, "What is a self-assessment?" sets forth a simple, straightforward guide through the self-assessment process.[1] Among other things, the article asks readers to identify their values, interests, motivational drives, what they are good at, and what they enjoy.

Consider whether to use some of the information obtained from the material you gather for your personal branding exercise. Your self-assessment should include:

- What you think of or know about yourself;
- The feedback you have received from others; and
- Your personality traits.

Next, review the feedback you have requested. After thoughtful consideration, if you agree with the feedback, keep it in mind when you complete a self-assessment test. The data you gathered and agree with should be emphasized in your marketing pitch, résumés, cover letters, and during job interviews.

---

[1] McKay, D.R. 2019. "Self-Assessment, An Overview." Blog, *thebalancecareers*. Updated June 25, 2019, https://thebalancecareers.com/self-assessment-524753

Pay attention to details. Everything must be consistent, so you convey that you are a confident, well-prepared professional who is exactly the person to fill the open position or to be promoted.

You will find the Occupational Information Network (O*NET)[2] useful as you develop your career plan. O*NET is sponsored by the U.S. Department of Labor/Employment and Training Administration. The website's database also provides career exploration tools for people who are looking to find or change careers.

These tools will assist in determining the career path that will be most gratifying based on your interests and skillset. The objective at this early point in your career is to be your own career coach.

Later in your career, if you feel that you have hit a plateau, or you simply want to move further up the company hierarchy, you may choose to hire a professional career coach. Your decision will depend on your career goals and finances.

When considering a career path, do not overlook entrepreneurial and/or vocational careers. These service-related occupations including the building trades (e.g., carpenters, plumbers, and electricians), auto-body and repair work, and personal-appearance workers (e.g., barbers, hairdressers, makeup artists, and manicurists) usually require on-the-job, hands-on training. Vocational programs neither cost as much as academic programs nor take as long to complete. Apprenticeship programs and community colleges are cost-saving options to be considered instead of, in addition to, or until you can afford a four-year college.

Furthermore, the tasks performed by vocational businesses are not likely to be computerized, automated, or outsourced. In 2014, economic indicators accurately predicted that the shortage of skilled craft professionals would continue. Although the housing and real estate industries are recovering, more skilled workers are retiring from the building trades.[3]

---

[2] The O*NET Online. https://onetonline.org/

[3] Chamberlain, S. 2019. "Addressing the Skilled Labor Shortage in America." Blog, *Forbes,* August 21, 2019, https://forbes.com/sites/sarahchamberlain/2019/08/21/addressing-the-skilled-labor-shortage-in-america/?sh=5910b23a181d; Ferriere, T. Trade School Careers: High Demand Job Opportunities for Graduates, https://intercoast.edu/blog/trade-school-careers/

It is not surprising that building-industry groups are engaged in developing future construction industry leaders. Given that the path to vocational career employment opportunities is often more attainable than other career paths, it makes sense to consider whether a vocational business or occupation might suit you and your interests.

As you review self-assessment and career-path material, consider the following eight questions:

1. What are my goals?
2. Am I willing to take the steps necessary to achieve my goals?
3. Where do I want to be in three and five years?
4. What kind of skills and experience do I need to achieve my goals?
5. Do I need skills that I do not have?
6. Do I need additional education and training?
7. Will I need to relocate to achieve my goals?
8. Who will accompany me on my journey?[4]

To answer the last question honestly, you will need to have the answers to the previous seven questions. Accordingly, before you choose a career and develop a career plan, it will be necessary to conduct research to acquire the information and data that will enable you to make an informed decision and set attainable career goals.

You may want to be successful but, as emphasized previously, achieving success takes hard work, focus, commitment, and talent, and the ability to take advantage of each opportunity. Think about whether you are sincerely willing to do the work and make the sacrifices necessary to achieve your goals. Be prepared to face negative feedback, delays, and other goal-limiting experiences that may shatter your resolve and self-esteem.

You will be able to use the answers to these eight questions and the research data to help you complete your self-assessment tool. Realize that

---

[4] See *e.g.,* Indeed Career Guide, The 8-Step Career-Planning Process, November 30, 2020 The 8-Step Career-Planning Process https://indeed.com/career-advice/career-development/career-planning-process; See, also Powell, C.L. n.d. "The Less You Associate with Some People the More Your Life Will Improve." https://goodreads.com/quotes/310930-the-less-you-associate-with-some-people-the-more-your

some of these items will change over time as you gain work-related and other experience.

Similarly, some goals and values will become more important to you later than they were when you began. Also acknowledge that the converse may be true. Later in life, for better or worse, these aspirations may not resonate as they do now.

The depth to which you address the first question will make your answer to the second question easier to visualize. A word of caution: You may not be comfortable with your answer to the eighth question, "Who will accompany me on my journey?"

It is said that

> ...you're the product of the five people you spend time with. If you allow even one of those five people to be toxic, you'll soon find out how capable he or she is of holding you back.[5]

Toxic people deplete your energy, time, and create stress. Learn to identify and avoid such individuals.

If anyone you are close to, whether family, friend, loved one, or associates, is "toxic," re-evaluate the relationship. Decide whether you can create distance between them and you so that you can move forward productively. *10 Toxic People You Should Avoid Like the Plague* is the name of the online source that describes the characteristics of toxic people.[6]

### TIP 5-69 Take inventory.
A quotation from Colin Powell, 65th Secretary of State of the United States and a retired four-star general in the U.S. Army, contains the following sage advice:

> The less you associate with some people, the more your life will improve. Any time you tolerate mediocrity in others, it increases

---

[5] Dr. Bradberry, T., Contributor. 2017. "10 Toxic People You Should Avoid Like the Plague." Blog, *HuffPost*, Updated May 13, 2017, https://huffpost.com/entry/10-toxic-people-you-should-avoid-like-the-plague_b_591344f2e4b07e366cebb80e

[6] Ibid.; 10 Toxic People You Should Avoid Like the Plague, Blog, Lolly Daskal, https://lollydaskal.com/leadership/10-toxic-people-avoid-like-plague/

your mediocrity. An important attribute in successful people is their impatience with negative thinking and negative acting people.

... Don't follow anyone who's not going anywhere ... With some people you spend an evening, with others you invest it ... If you run with wolves, you will learn how to howl. But, if you associate with eagles, you will learn how to soar to great heights ...

... Never make someone a priority when you are only an option for them.[7]

The previous paragraphs are merely excerpts from a lengthy quotation from Secretary Powell. His quotation also addresses the role that family plays in your future plans, and applies the standard that is used for both friends and family members. You can benefit from reading the entire quotation and taking time to think about its meaning for you.

Of course, family members will be on the journey with you, although the influence each family member has on you will vary. You may want to determine which family members are best equipped to provide advice and counsel on how to achieve your goals successfully.

Do not make the mistake of equating success with the mere acquisition of wealth, status, a lot of "bling," or a corner office on the top floor of corporate headquarters. People who are honest, hardworking, and respectful of and respected by others are individuals from whom you can learn and who may have helpful advice.

To answer the eighth question adequately, you will need to evaluate the people you know and with whom you come in contact with to ascertain what, if any, role they will or should have in your forward-moving progress. Ideally, you will want to surround yourself with people who are positive, reliable, and trustworthy—people who exercise sound judgment and have integrity, are ethical, and who support you.

Because of their relationship to you or your affection for them, family members and friends may be the most difficult individuals to evaluate. For example, a cousin you grew up with, who has substance abuse

---

[7] Powell, C.L. n.d. "The Less You Associate with Some People the More Your Life Will Improve." https://goodreads.com/quotes/310930-the-less-you-associate-with-some-people-the-more-your

problems and a propensity for criminal or inappropriate conduct, is not someone you will probably spend a great deal of time with discussing your plans for the future. Likewise, you will have to decide how to handle friends who want to party 24/7 or who are going nowhere fast.

You may also need to think about whether to keep your constantly complaining sister or brother-in-law at arm's length because he or she is so negative and snarky. You love them, but you are on a mission.

**Do not get it twisted:** You should not leave family and friends behind because they hit a rough patch or do not share your values and plans for the future.

- Loved ones who, over time, have demonstrated their love, support, and encouragement for you are your bridges to the future.
- If by chance you achieve success, you may not enjoy it as much without such people in your life; you will, however, need to manage these relationships.

If you cannot say "no" to friends who want to party until the wee hours on a weeknight when you have to work or look for work the next day, do not talk to them during the week. Save your conversations and time together for the weekend.

A relative, who is dear to you and who has biases that you do not share (or do not freely reveal), may not understand if you befriend coworkers who are "different" from you. Unfortunately, even in the 21st century, there are people who are intolerant of differences in, among other things, race, religion, and sexual expression.

Also, consider whether it is wise to invite that relative to join you and a diverse group of coworkers at the local sports bar to watch the Super Bowl. Think of it as if you were assigning seats at each table at a wedding reception. You do not seat Aunt Maude next to Uncle Rupert because they hate each other. You seat Cousin Melanie as far away as possible from her ex-husband Ethan and his new wife, a 21-year-old professional cheerleader.

Ultimately, it is your responsibility to manage your personal and professional relationships to your advantage, so you do not derail your plans for the future. Take into account your values, skills, goals, ethics, interests, and current passions. Avoid the pursuit of a career that someone else chooses for you.

*Luis earned an undergraduate degree from an Ivy League college. His father wanted him to become an attorney, so, being a dutiful son, Luis graduated from a top-tier law school. He practiced law for more than 15 years before he declared that he had never wanted to be an attorney and left the practice of law. Thereafter, he pursued his passion for journalism and graduated from a highly regarded graduate school of journalism.*

You need to understand yourself, your goals, and aspirations in order to maximize your chance for success. Begin by objectively identifying your strengths and weaknesses. Admittedly, it is difficult to be objective about yourself. Nonetheless, try. Ask yourself thoughtful, probing questions in an effort to identify the career path best for you.

**Strengths and Weaknesses**

No matter what your loved ones tell you, you are not perfect. You have weaknesses, but you also have strengths. We all have them, and interviewers usually ask applicants to identify theirs.

Thus, it is important that you practice describing your strengths and weaknesses. If you are self-aware and able to articulate this information succinctly and coherently without presenting yourself in a negative light, you will increase your interviewing success.

**TIP 5-70 Develop a plan and execute it.**

**Career plan:** It is time to connect the dots. Your career plan should include developmental goals and timetables to:

- Direct your journey to find a job;
- Determine whether you are on track to achieve your goals;
- Determine whether you need to reassess the long-term benefit of remaining with your current plan; and
- Determine whether your plan should be revised.

Your goals and objectives should be:

- Reasonable;
- Realistic;

- Achievable; and
- Directed toward a due date or within a certain time frame.

Every career plan should include steps to establish, expand, and maintain face-to-face and online social networks.

**Example 1:** You have a bachelor's degree in liberal arts from an accredited college, but you do not have a clue about what you want to be now that you are out of school or ready to change careers.

Your interests are varied:

- You enjoy participating in outdoor sports, watching professional and collegiate sports on television (either at home or at sport bars), listening to music, and "kicking back" with friends.
- You do not view yourself as a leader or a follower.
- You consider yourself an independent thinker.
- You are not interested in recognition.
- You are more interested in getting things done.
- You are relatively inexperienced and know that you may need to be flexible about work schedules, including the hours and days you make yourself available to work.

You have already completed a personality assessment to help determine what your preferences are and to learn more about yourself. Based on your personality assessment, you are a responsible extrovert who is in touch with your external environment.

You now complete a career assessment to guide you toward a career choice. According to your career assessment and based on your limited work experience, you may find a customer service or a sales position rewarding.

## Sample Career Plan

- Learn the requirements for call center and sales positions by reviewing job descriptions on O*NET.
- Expand your network of people beyond social networks by joining professional organizations (if you can afford it) and volunteering in your community.
- By (date), identify the businesses that have call centers and sales organizations and their locations.

- By (date), identify the states that have the lowest rates of unemployment.
- By (date), communicate with friends and relatives in these states for networking contacts and opportunities.
- Contact your alumni, job placement, and unemployment offices for contacts.

**Example 2:** Status (e.g., a high salary and recognition) is important to you. You do not have a degree. These are values you should include on your list:

- You enjoy bowling, skiing, and music. These are the things that interest you.
- You are outgoing, analytical, and typically a person who is the life of the party.
- Teaching has always appealed to you because it is an opportunity to share your point of view.
- You are a skilled debater who communicates clearly, concisely, and simply.

Your values appear to be in conflict with your skill set—but maybe not. You can become a teacher or a college professor if you are willing to acquire a degree or two. It may mean acquiring a graduate degree if you plan to teach at the college level.

If you really want to teach, and money and status are important to you, establish additional revenue streams to supplement your teaching income and to distinguish yourself as a teacher or in some other way. It will take planning and a lot of work, but it can be done.

To establish additional revenue streams as a teacher, you may:

- Coach an intermural sport or activity; and/or
- Tutor students in subjects in which you are proficient and that you enjoy.

You may achieve the status you want by:

- Becoming active in professional organizations; and
- Running for office in the organization.

If you are so inclined, and either have the talent or are willing to develop it, you may also become a motivational or public speaker. Obviously, it takes time and experience to become a successful speaker with a message worth hearing, but it can be done—especially if you are passionate about your subject and committed to your objectives.

## Sample Career Plan

- By (date), identify a college or university with evening classes, and plan to enroll as a part-time student to acquire a bachelor's degree.
- If you cannot afford to attend school, ask for permission to audit a class for a couple of weeks as a nonmatriculating student. Hopefully, this experience should either confirm that you want to continue with your education or that you should consider another direction.
- Determine which colleges offer bachelor's degrees that will permit you to teach in public schools immediately upon graduation.
- Apply for admission to a college or colleges within commuting distance from your home.
- Consider math or science as a major. (There is always a market for these areas.)
- Research programs, such as Teach America, and determine whether this type of program suits you and your plans for the future.

**Example 3:** You want to become an attorney. You have a bachelor's degree and considerable student-loan debt. You need to work, but becoming a lawyer is your passion.

**Career-plan proposal:** As you continue to look for employment, and depending on whether you end up working full time during the day or at night:

- Determine whether there is a law school (a state school will likely cost less for state residents) within commuting distance and whether it has an evening program; and

- Consider relocating to that state and establishing residency while continuing your job search.

After you have found a job, find out whether your employer offers tuition assistance; if not, explore attending law school in the evening as a part-time student and working full time during the day, or working nights and attending law school during the day.

### TIP 5-71 Remember: There is nothing like the prospect of success and prosperity.

Whatever your goals and ambitions are, you are on your way to achieving success, as you define it, and hopefully prosperity. You want to position yourself so that you have and can make choices. Likewise, you want to make decisions on the job that will not negatively impact your ability to earn a comfortable living and a productive life.

Once again, persistence, tenacity, and common sense are essential to achieve positive results. Without them, you are not likely to be successful in a competitive job market.

### TIP 5-72 Whether you are employed or unemployed, attention to detail is essential.

When your supervisor gives you an assignment, listen carefully and repeat your understanding of what must be done. The due date, time, format, and anything else relevant to getting the job done exactly as your supervisor specifies or directs are essential elements for ensuring on-the-job success. Confirming the assignment in writing increases both your and your supervisor's understanding.

If the date and time are not provided, ask for them. Also ask if there are any special instructions about the presentation of the assignment. It is important to know how to please your supervisor with the work you are assigned. The level of your expectations is also important because unmet expectations make for dissatisfied, unhappy, unproductive employees.

For job searchers, making sure that résumés and cover letters do not have typographical errors and contain consistent information is critically important. Attention to detail is one of the keys to your career success. Ask a good writer to review your work.

## CHAPTER 6

# You're Looking for a Job ....
# They Don't Call It Work
# for Nothing!

*Each generation goes further than the generation preceding
it because it stands on the shoulders of that generation. You
will have opportunities beyond anything we've ever known.*

—Ronald Reagan,
40th president of the United States

*Opportunity is missed by most people because it
is dressed in overalls and looks like work.*

—Thomas Alva Edison,
inventor

You may not realize it, but you already have a job. Looking for a job is
your job. In previous chapters, to set expectations, you were encouraged to
spend as much time each day on your job search as you would spend working on a full-time job. Work, effort, diligence, networking, and attention to
detail are all words that should describe your job-search efforts.

The first thing to do is organize yourself, especially your thoughts. Next:

- Consider the materials you will need.
- Identify the documents you will need.
- Create a list of people you plan to contact.
- This list should expand as your network grows.
- Maintain a record of whom you contact, what you send them, when you sent it, and whether and when follow-up is necessary.

**Research:** Information is a powerful tool. Research the businesses and organizations to which you plan to submit résumés. Then, become totally familiar with what you learn. Your objective is to distinguish yourself—to stand out when compared to other applicants.

As you survey the market, you want to gather information to best determine whether an industry or a particular employer will be a good fit for you. A "good fit" includes employers and positions that require talent that aligns with your skillset, experience, educational background, and interests. If you apply for employment, be assured that an employer will make the same assessment. Will you fit the company's culture?

Ideally, it is also employment that you genuinely believe will keep you engaged and interested in the work you will be expected to perform. Assess the aptitudes that are necessary, including the skills and training required.

Determine whether the business culture of the industry and employer suits your personality and work style. A systematic, diligent investigation and assessment of the fit of an industry and a particular prospective employer, including their reputation, are in order.

Research and networking will reduce the likelihood that you will be surprised or land in a position that does not mesh well with your skillset, goals, and interests. This will best prepare you to be most effective in the interviewing process and help you screen out situations where the culture and job fit will not be in your best interest.

Follow prospective employers online, on social networks, on television and radio, and in trade publications that pertain to the industries, businesses, and organizations in your areas of interest. Often, these publications contain listings for job openings. They also provide information about companies, such as whether they are laying off employees or planning to increase staff. Be sure to keep your focus on potential employers that you want to work for and that might be interested in your skillset.

Two important directories to review are:

- The Directory of Associations, which lists all associations/ organizations and their departments, principal officers, and contact information
- The Directory of Executive & Professional Recruiters, which provides a comprehensive listing of recruiters and each firm's specialty, including contact information

These directories may be available at college career centers and public libraries. If they do not have them, find the organizations on the Internet, contact them directly, and tell whoever responds that you are looking for a job and cannot afford to pay for the directory.

Ask for assistance but remember that they are not obligated to help you. Perhaps whomever you speak to can give you the name of a local contact who may let you use a directory.

Additionally, you should:

- Conduct an Internet search of your area of experience, expertise, or interest. You will probably identify unfamiliar publications, persons, and firms that can be helpful to you.
- Make a list of material pertinent to your area of interest, including contact possibilities.
- Contact professional organizations in your field and attend their meetings. These organizations often hold meetings that provide networking opportunities. You can never have too many leads.
- Prepare a list of career job sites that are applicable to your field as well as sites that are more general.
- Make it a habit to check these sites every day and apply for positions for which you are qualified. It is important to check

them regularly, but do not spend too much time on these
sites.[1]

- For reviews of employers and businesses, *"18 Employer Review
Sites to Put on Your Radar"* identifies "popular and emerging"
websites that provide employer reviews.

Admittedly, you have a great deal to do. Organization will help, but do
not neglect the maintenance of an up-to-date backup of your job-search
materials. If something is misplaced or lost, your backup will save the day.

Next, make a list of the items you need:

- References
  - Identify the people you plan to ask to give you professional
    and personal references.
  - Request the proper spelling of their names and titles. If
    possible, obtain business and cell phone numbers and
    e-mail and business addresses.
  - Make sure to contact these people to ask them if they will
    give you a reference.
  - Do not presume that they will.
  - If they agree, discuss what they plan to say about you.
  - Make sure to send a thank you note or e-mail.
- Résumés (different formats)
- Cover letters
- Network contact list, including the names of people to
  contact
- A deep background check on yourself to discover what it
  contains and to verify its accuracy
- Writing sample or sample presentation

The items listed above should be in final form before you begin your
job search because you will want to send out material as soon as you get

---

[1] Thanks to Martha Sloane, Principal, MARTHA SLOANE CONSULTANTS,
LTD, a recruiting firm, Greater New York City Area, for her contribution to this
section.

a job lead. A list will keep you organized as well as help you prepare for interviews and send follow-up thank you letters.

You may decide to include additional items on your list, but you get the idea. Now that you have prepared a list of tasks that you need to perform to find your next position, set a goal for yourself. For example, your goal might be that you will send out a certain number of résumés and make a certain number of calls each weekday.

**Remember:** People cannot hire you if they do not know you are available.

### TIP 6-73 Seek employment with employers who encourage and value ethics and integrity.

"Ethics" means different things to different people. At its foundation, it is the belief that people should conduct themselves with honesty and integrity.

The aim of the public sector is to serve people, but private sector enterprises are established with a profit motive. Similarly, many corporations, organizations, and especially government entities create strong mission statements to establish strict company values and ethics.[2]

These values and ethics set the tone, framework, and character for the organizations and its employees.[3] There are shades of gray where ethical considerations are involved, but the gray areas should not cross the line into the clearly wrong province.

Regardless of the position you seek or have and how much or how little money you earn, honesty and integrity are important. "When you barely make enough to live, being able to live with yourself means a lot more."[4]

The objective of your employment search is to have a successful career with an employer who is, among other things, profitable, stable, and ethical. If the nonprofit world interests you, look for organizations whose mission statements and track record align with your goals and interests.

---

[2] Johnson, D.T. 2019. "The Importance of Ethics in Public Service." *PA Times,* June 2, 2019, https://patimes.org/the-importance-of-ethics-in-public-service/
[3] Ibid.
[4] Jones, B. 2020. "The Game." *Vanity Fair,* September 2020, https://archive.vanityfair.com/article/2020/9/the-game

The research you conduct about prospective employers should give you some indication of the profitability and stability of the company. Your research should be creative and expansive.

Check published reports online and court records to look for indications that raise ethical or other troubling concerns. Make a trip or telephone call to your local federal court to find out how you can obtain the information you want.

After you are hired, pay attention to whether there is conduct in the workplace that may be unethical. For example, if you hear phrases that describe your employer's workplace as "an audit-rich environment," consider the description "a red flag" which may indicate that there may be an ethical or legal issue.

**Do not get it twisted:** Do not rush to judgment. Do not conclude that your employer is disreputable based only on what may be a stray comment. Rather, pay attention to what goes on around you, and make plans as the situation dictates. Try to find out more by monitoring online references to your company.

### TIP 6-74 Do not appear desperate when interviewing for a job.

When you arrive for a job interview, it is a given that you are interested in a specific position. As an applicant, you want to be confident about your strengths and be able to articulate your weaknesses and how you are working on them. Look at the personal branding and self-assessment work you have done to identify your strengths and weaknesses.

You are aware that the employer holds all the cards or power, but you want to try to level the playing field. If you have marketable skills that are unique or in demand, you may be positioned to negotiate a higher salary, additional fringe benefits, and other perquisites.

Perhaps your financial situation necessitates that you find a job as quickly as possible to avoid dire predicaments. If that is not the case, consider this approach: Tell the interviewer that you are interested in learning about the position. Also say that you want to make sure that this is the right job for you, and that you are the right person for the job, because you are looking for a role that will permit you to make a substantive contribution. You do not think that is likely to happen if you are a square peg in a round hole.

If you do not think the current economy is the most propitious time to use this approach, put it in your arsenal for use later in your career when you are in a better position to use it.

**TIP 6-75 Seriously consider a temporary position.**
Ask yourself whether you should wait around for a permanent position that may not come for a year or more. Temporary or "nonstandard" workers—otherwise known as *gig,* independent contractors, contingent workers, and freelancers—do not receive health insurance, retirement benefits, sick and vacation days, severance, or unemployment benefits—but they do get paid.

Terminology aside, the number of temporary workers that create the "gig economy" is growing. Whether because employers seek to avoid hiring full-time employees and paying attendant fringe benefits or because of the disappearance of job security, individuals are pursuing different paths to achieve employment stability.[5]

Federal and state laws attempt to prevent the illegal, abusive use of temporary workers. The abuses continue, nonetheless. If you accept a temporary position, you may find yourself thrust into a situation that requires you to make a decision.

**Consider this scenario:** You have been employed as a temporary worker continuously, without a break in service, for two and one-half years. You have not received health benefits. You find out that, under federal and state laws, you may be legally considered an employee and therefore entitled to benefits during some of that time.

Do you go to your supervisor or the federal or state departments of labor, or do you continue to work under your current circumstances?

Here are some suggestions:

- Contact the federal and state departments of labor in your state anonymously, tell them your story, and inquire about your status.
- Call several other U.S. Department of Labor offices in other states to see if the answers about federal law are consistent.

---

[5] Longley, R. 2019. "Gig Economy: Definition and Pros and Cons." Blog, *Thought Co,* Updated March 15, 2019, https://thoughtco.com/gig-economy-4588490

- Ask for and write down the names of everyone to whom you speak.
- Do not disclose your name or identify your employer or supervisor.
- Do not place the call from work, home, or where caller identification can identify the source. You are merely on an information-gathering mission.

Before you decide what to do, make sure that you have adequate information to make an informed decision. If you complain, your employer might terminate your employment. If you were employed in violation of wage and hour laws, you may be entitled to return to your position with back pay, but it could take weeks, months, or even longer.

### TIP 6-76 Looking for a job takes work (e.g., time, effort, focus, and follow-up).

*Opportunities are usually disguised by hard work, so most people don't recognize them.*

—Ann Landers,
advice columnist

Once you make the commitment to put in the time and effort required, how you conduct your job search will depend on your financial situation. Varying economic circumstances will necessarily result in different approaches and a different mindset. If, however, you are a step away from homelessness, anxiety and desperation are difficult to mask.

Not at the end of your rope? If you are in the position to do so:

- Select businesses at which you would like to work.
- Visualize what you want your working environment to look like.
  - Are there offices, cubicles, or open spaces?
  - Is the available position located in the city or the suburbs?
  - How will you get to work? Make sure you have an alternate plan.
  - How are employees dressed? Is there a dress code?

- Imagine how you want a typical workday to feel.
- Think about whom you might know who works there.
- If you do not know anyone, visit the business in advance and try to speak to employees. Ask them what they like about the company and why. If security limits access, try to find employees online.

## At the End of Your Rope?

*When you come to the end of your rope, tie a knot, and hang on.*
—Franklin D. Roosevelt,
32nd president of the United States

You are networking, have been on interviews with no success, and are about to be evicted from your home. You can persuasively articulate your experience, skills, and attributes because you have been practicing. Here are some ideas about what to do next:

- Armed with copies of your résumé, hit the streets, restaurants, shopping and strip malls, and large retail stores that are not in malls.
- Politely and professionally ask to speak to the manager.
- With a smile and a nod, look the manager in the eye and tell him or her that you need work and why, and that you will do any (legal) job to earn a living. (Do not say it if you do not mean it!)
- If the manager is unavailable, ask politely when he or she will be available. Wait, if you can.
- While you are waiting, talk to the employees and anyone else who is around, and tell them that you are looking for work because your circumstances are dire.
- You must be persistent and relentless. Do not lose heart.

Another approach is to turn your passion or avocation into a paying job by using what you have and doing what you can. You may be able to create a job based on a need that has not been met or a problem for which you have an appealing solution. Creating multiple income streams and turning a revenue-generating venture into a job are examples of how creative people can be in trying times.

*An unemployed man, who was passionate about environmental issues as well as active in his community, followed his passion and vocation by leading neighborhood cleanups and various types of environmental remediation.*

*His passion for his work gained the attention of several local universities and government officials at various levels. The resulting collaboration led to an offer of employment from the local government's environmental business partner. He worked himself into a job based on a need that he found in his community.*

**TIP 6-77 Résumés must be complete, concise, accurate, neat, and easy to read.**

**TIP 6-78 Your résumé should contain key words and phrases that will help identify you as a potential candidate.**
To maximize the likelihood that you will be considered for jobs that require the same skill set, but with varying emphasis on these skill sets, you will need more than one version of your résumé. The emphasis will be different, but the data should be the same so that, when you are interviewed, you present yourself as a well-prepared, confident professional regardless of the job you seek.

All of your contact information should appear at the top of your résumé and should include your name, home address, home phone number (if you have one), cell phone number, and e-mail address. You want to make it easy for the reader to contact you.

If you have been out of work for an extended period, or want to change careers, your résumé should emphasize experience and attributes that make you an attractive candidate for the position you want.

With so many people actively looking for employment, your marketing pitch, résumé, and cover letter will need to be exceptional. If you deviate from the expected résumé format, you may send a red flag that you are trying to hide something.

To the extent you can, your résumé should:

- Use an easy-to-read font, such as Times New Roman, with 11- or 12-point type.

- Have an easy-to-read bulleted format, which is usually preferred by recruiters and executives.
- Limit your résumé to one or two pages.
- Highlight your employment experience and education.
- The body of the résumé should:
  - Start with your most recent job.
  - List additional employment chronologically beginning with the next most recent job if you had one.
  - For each job listed, include a brief description of your responsibilities and achievements.
  - Next, list your education and date of graduation as well as any awards you have received and volunteer work.
  - Last, list your computer skills and any other skills and training you have.
- When completing résumés and employment applications, as previously stated, it is important to pay attention to details.
  - Dates are important, so do not guess about them if you can avoid it.
  - If necessary, and for the sake of accuracy, look for documents that will help you reconstruct your prior employment history, addresses, and educational information.
  - Never include inaccurate or embellished information on your résumé.
  - If you are unsure of a date, name, or address, indicate your uncertainty by using "approximately" or "approx." on your résumé or employment application.
  - If you need two pages because you cannot reasonably include all your employers, education, and other relevant information on one page, use two pages.
  - Avoid anything that may indicate that you have not provided complete, accurate information.

Recruiters use computer-generated database searches, which focus on keywords and phrases found in job descriptions. Typically, keywords are used in management theories and concepts.

Accordingly, your résumé should contain words and phrases that appear in the job description of the position for which you are applying. For example, if the description says that the employer is looking for a candidate who can be a "strategic partner" or someone with a "proven track record," "analytic capability," or "leadership skills," these phrases should be used to describe you—either through the jobs you held previously or through nonwork-related activities and your personality.

As you progress with your job search, depending on the position you are applying for, you may find that you will need to create multiple versions of your résumé in order to emphasize different skills.

Be prepared to tailor your résumé to each job description. Here are a few additional items to keep in mind:

- Be sure that your résumé is accurate and proofread before you submit it.
- If you know an HR professional, ask her or him to evaluate your résumé.
- Résumés must be neat and contain no typos. Someone other than you should proofread it before you distribute it.

**TIP 6-79 Include a cover letter with your résumé unless you are told not to do so.**
Your cover letter should:

- Identify you and the job for which you are applying.
- Describe why you are interested in the position, and how you would be an asset and add value.
- If applicable, identify the person who referred you.

If the recruiter does not want a cover letter, it can be discarded. Consider this rule of thumb: When in doubt, follow tradition. Put another way, it is better to have and not need than to need and not have.

It is not necessary to provide much detail, but you will want to list some of the skills you have that meet the requirements of the position. You also want to keep it short and interesting. Also, make sure it is well written. The objective is to make the reader interested enough to read your résumé and invite you in for an in-person interview or at least a telephone interview.

**Interviewing:** Consider the questions you may be asked and practice your answers. Ask intelligent questions, which you sincerely want answered and which demonstrate that you have taken the time to prepare for your interview.

**Preparation:** The Internet has resources that provide sample interview questions. Practice answering these questions. Reportedly, interview questions found on the Internet have been known to be used in actual interviews.

You do not want to miss an opportunity to shine in an interview simply because you did not take the time to check out the resources identified for you. Practice, practice, practice!

**Video[6] and telephone interviews:** If you think that because video and telephone interviews are less formal than in-person interviews, you can take a more relaxed approach to preparing for and participating in the interview, you are wrong.

These formats are commonly used to screen or narrow the field of candidates, and then eliminate those who do not pass the screener's criteria for moving to the next step. Think of it this way: Your résumé and cover letter are your calling cards. Video and telephone interviews are your qualifying round for the main event: an in-person interview.

Obviously, the most significant difference between a telephone interview and an in-person interview is that the interviewer and interviewee do not see each other. Accordingly, unless it is a video conference, what you wear is not important. How you sound, what you say, and how you say it are extremely important.

Remember to smile and maintain eye contact during video conferences. Additionally,

- Get out of bed at least two hours before the interview begins, so you do not sound sleepy or have a "morning" voice.

---

[6] The Best Way to Set Up for a Video Interview (So You'll Look and Sound Like a Winning Candidate), Regina Borsellino, https://themuse.com/advice/how-to-prepare-for-video-interview

- Drink something hot to clear your throat.
- Eat a light breakfast that will not leave you sluggish.
- Present yourself as awake and engaged.
- During the interview, you may want to stand or walk around if you can remain focused and answer questions clearly.
- If you cannot remain focused, sit at a desk or table.

An advantage to a telephone interview is that you can take notes; however, do not try to take detailed notes. Limit note-taking to one or two words as a reminder for follow-up later in the interview.

Do not do anything during a telephone interview that you would not do during an in-person interview. Take this advice seriously. A successful telephone interview will move you to the next step.

*Amy was thoroughly prepared for her telephone interview with a staffing coordinator of ABC Products, Inc., a global company with offices in several countries. She used the company's personal-care products, loved its commercials, and was impressed by its mission statement and commitment to environmental issues. The more Amy learned about the company, the more positive she became that she wanted to land a position at ABC Products.*

*Amy was ready for her telephone interview because she had reviewed her research multiple times and had perfected her marketing pitch. She knew that she had to ace this interview in order to be invited for a face-to-face interview.*

*Unfortunately, Amy had forgotten to use the bathroom before the telephone interview began. When she could put it off no longer, Amy not only used the toilet, she flushed it.*

*Guess what? She did not get to the next step. No face-to-face interview for Amy.*

Just because you cannot be seen does not mean you cannot be heard.

**How to dress for an interview:** Take the time to research the prospective employer's dress code and business culture to determine how best to present yourself. As previously advised, be true to yourself and your personal style, if you are unwilling to adapt. There may be consequences.

If you have visible body piercings, tattoos, and/or vibrantly colored hair, and you are unwilling to remove the piercings, wear clothing that covers the tats, and dye your hair a more conventional color, do not look for a job at businesses that does not embrace your personal style.

Your research should provide that information. If you have decided that you are willing to adopt the company's culture, do not change your manner of dress drastically after you are hired.

Whatever you wear should be clean and well pressed. The objective is to present yourself as a pulled together, knowledgeable person with an appropriate appearance.

*Helen arrived for an interview dressed in black yoga pants with a matching jacket and high heels. She chose to accessorize this outfit with a graphic T-shirt and six studded earrings in each ear. Her eye shadow was electric blue. The interviewer told Helen that she was not qualified for the job. She also explained as gently as possible that Helen did not present a professional image and gave her some tips on dressing appropriately for job interviews.*

Hopefully, Helen took the interviewer's advice.

**The interview:** First and foremost, you must know your résumé cold, inside, and out. If you cannot, with an engaging smile, comfortably and confidently discuss your background with interviewers, why should they hire you?

You must be able to convince anyone that, because of your maturity, willingness to work hard, and eagerness to learn, you are the person for the job. Make sure to set aside adequate time for your interview and come alone. If others must come with you, leave them at a nearby restaurant or store. You must not be distracted.

Whether you have applied for a job with your current employer or are unemployed and looking for a new position, prepare for interviews by updating and reviewing your original research about the business, division, or supervisor, and the position you seek.

Review annual reports, business summaries, and articles, all of which you can obtain by conducting an Internet search. Even when you feel that you are ready, practice, practice, practice.

If you are an applicant, determine whether this is the company you want to work for by paying attention when you are on premises for the interview. This will verify the accuracy of your research about the business. Are the following considerations important to you?

- Do you see indications that the employer recycles?
- Is there material about environmental matters on bulletin boards?

- If diversity is important to you, do you see people of various nationalities and ethnicities?
- Is there a balance of men and women?
- Do you notice any disabled employees?

At the end of the interview, thank interviewers for their time and ask the people whom you meet for their business cards.

*When Jane arrived for her interview with a small company's office manager, she was anxious and somewhat abrupt with the receptionist. Her behavior was understandable because she had come to the job interview with her child and her sister.*

*During the interview, Jane asked the office manager how much longer the interview would take. She explained that her sister had driven her to the interview rather than allowing her to use her car because Jane has a history of not returning the car as promised. Jane's interview was also interrupted when the receptionist knocked on the door to inform her that her child was throwing mini tantrums.*

Jane did not get the job.

*Mary arrived at the interview and asked if her husband could join them. The interviewer declined the request and advised Mary that she would prefer to have a one-on-one interview.*

*Mary told the interviewer that her husband was very impatient, and that she needed to inform him of the time frame for the interview. According to Mary, her husband was going to leave and come back for her at the conclusion of the interview, but he needed an exact time, as he was very inflexible.*

*The interviewer told Mary that she did not know, and she was free to continue the interview or leave with her husband. The husband decided to wait but sighed and tapped his foot the entire time he waited in the reception area.*

Mary did not get the job.

*An interviewer asked why a law school graduate wanted to become an attorney. The answer that Perry Mason, a television criminal drama that originally aired from 1957 to 1966, again from 1985 to 1995, and reruns later on cable TV, had inspired her, though true, did not land well. The expression on the interviewer's face conveyed the message.*

*The law school graduate was not hired. She learned, however, to respond more thoughtfully to interview questions.*

What is the moral of these stories? Never bring anyone with you to the interview, set aside the entire day so you do not appear rushed, and provide an intelligent, professional, sensible reason for wanting the position.

Depending on the jurisdiction, employers may ask questions that elicit information about:

- Business cultural fit
- Motivation
- Behavior
- Leadership
- Management skills
- Interpersonal skills
- Teams and teamwork
- Whether you are legally able to work in the United States

Employers should not ask personal questions, which are unrelated to the applicant's ability to do the job, such as:

- What is your race?
- What is your national origin?
- What is your gender?
- What is your religion?
- Do you plan to have children?
- How old are you?
- Do you have a disability?
- What is your sexual orientation or gender identity?
- What is your marital status?
- How old are your children?
- What arrangements are you able to make for childcare while you work?
- When did you graduate from high school?
- Are you a U.S. citizen?
- What does your spouse do for a living?
- Where did you live while you were growing up?
- Will you need personal time for particular religious holidays?

If you are asked a question that you think is inappropriate or even illegal, what should you do? You must decide.

- You can smile, look surprised, and say, "I was not expecting that question because my career counselor said it would not be asked."
- If you are willing to answer the question, tell the interviewer, "I'll answer the question if you want me to, but my career counselor said it would not be asked."
- If you are not willing to answer the question, politely say so and give a reason why.

**TIP 6-80 Always, always send a thank you letter or e-mail following an interview.**

Your thank you message should include language that informs the interviewer that he or she, and no one else, could have received this thank you because it specifically refers to topics discussed or mentioned during your interview.

Make sure the note thanks them for their time and lets them know how and why you would be an asset to the business and to the department.

Please do not forget to customize your thank you message by addressing the recipient by name. If you were told to call the interviewer by his or her first name, and did so during the interview, use "Dear ___"; otherwise, use "Mr." or "Ms."

## TIP 6-81 Face background-check problems head on.

After the tragic events of September 11, 2001, many employers whose businesses involve access to confidential, proprietary, or sensitive information, conduct background checks to identify undesirable candidates. The definition of "undesirable" varies from employer to employer.

If you apply for a sales position and need a valid driver's license, your background-check report will likely include your driving record. It is no surprise that applicants with driving while intoxicated or driving under the influence records and/or a high number of points may be bypassed for sales positions.

Consequently, do not consider any traffic violation minor. Be aware that talking or texting on your cell phone while driving may result in a "minor" violation that may show up on your background check. These infractions may prevent you from being hired for a sales position that requires driving and could affect your automobile insurance coverage.

Jobs in securities or other highly regulated industries are subject to stringent standards related to background checks. Thus, people who have been convicted of crimes that involve theft, fraud, and dishonesty are not likely to be hired in these industries.

**Background checks:** The information provided on your employment application is usually used to conduct your background check. If your new position involves access to confidential or sensitive data, you may be required to provide additional information.

You may also be asked to complete another document or supplement the information you have already provided. Take the steps necessary to make sure that the additional information you give is consistent with previously submitted information.

If you are denied employment because of information provided in your background check, you have a right to receive a copy of the background check report and the name, address, and phone number of the agency that provided the information. Additionally, you have the right to know what is in your file, and to dispute incomplete or inaccurate information.[7]

---

[7] A Summary of Your Rights Under the Fair Credit Reporting Act, https://consumer.ftc.gov/articles/pdf-0096-fair-credit-reporting-act.pdf

Note that questions permitted under federal law may be prohibited under state, county, or municipal jurisdictions. Additionally, in some jurisdictions, applicants cannot even be asked about arrests that did not result in conviction.[8]

**Convictions versus arrests:** On April 25, 2012, the Equal Employment Opportunity Commission (EEOC) issued its Enforcement Guidance on the Consideration of Arrest and Conviction Records in Employment Decisions Under Title VII of the Civil Rights Act of 1964 (Enforcement Guidance). http://eeoc.gov/laws/guidance/arrest_conviction.cfm. The EEOC seeks to ensure that arrest or conviction records are not used in a discriminatory way.

You should know that:

- Employers may inquire about past convictions because they are deemed reliable; and
- Employers may not inquire about previous arrests, which are considered less reliable.

Although the U.S. legal system presumes that a person is innocent until proven guilty, arrest records may appear on background checks. Do not panic. Just because you have an arrest record does not mean there is or was any merit to the charges. Similarly, because an employer can conduct a background check does not mean that the company can do anything it wants with what is learned about a prior arrest or conviction.

If you believe that an issue will surface in your background check, prepare a well-written explanation and practice delivering it, just in case you get an opportunity to explain. If possible, hold onto the explanation until after your interview, which hopefully you "aced." Submit your explanation to the hiring manager or the HR contact before you leave.

The person who reads your explanation may give you a chance to explain in person or to prove yourself on the job. If you do not provide

---

[8] See, Guerin, Lisa, "State Laws on Use of Arrests and Convictions in Employment" Blog, *NOLO* https://nolo.com/legal-encyclopedia/state-laws-use-arrests-convictions-employment.html; McLean, E. n.d. "Ban the Box." GoodHire Blog, https://goodhire.com/blog/ban-the-box/

an explanation, the background-check issue goes unanswered. The worst thing to do is to lie. The next worst thing to do is nothing. The employer will find out the truth eventually, and you may be discharged.

**Expunged conviction records:** Some convictions are eligible to be expunged or removed from the record. If an expungement procedure is initiated, confirm that your record has been cleared. You will appear dishonest if you fail to disclose a conviction that surfaces on your record.

As previously suggested, consider conducting your own background check through a reliable vendor before relying on a court order that directs the removal of the conviction from your record. Sometimes the act of removing the conviction is way behind the court order that directs the removal.

**Drug tests:** Generally, drug tests are conducted after an offer of employment is made. Whether entities may conduct or are required to conduct a drug test is governed by whether the employer is a private or public sector employer or a federal contractor.

The federal Drug-Free Workplace Act of 1988 provides that any employer who receives federal contracts or grants is required to maintain a drug-free working environment. If you are required to take a drug test, do not do what Mitchell did.

*In June 2020 in Nashville, Tennessee, ABC Company offered Mitchell a job contingent upon his successful completion of the company's pre-employment requirements, which included passing a drug test. To expedite Mitchell's start-to-work date, Judy, the HR director, offered to personally deliver the pre-employment package to Mitchell on her way home.*

*After Mitchell thanked Judy for her consideration, he then said, as if thinking out loud, "I hope that weed I smoked six months ago does not show up."*

*Judy did not know what to say. After Mitchell passed the drug test and began to work at ABC, Judy spoke to him about his statement. She told him that smoking "weed" and anything else that could be considered illegal conduct should not be discussed or mentioned to coworkers, and certainly not to a company HR professional. Hopefully, Mitchell realized that he had dodged a bullet.*

**TIP 6-82 If you are fortunate enough to have more than one offer, after you accept a written offer, notify other employers that you have accepted another offer.**

Once you have accepted a written offer, successfully passed all pre-employment requirements, and have a start-to-work date, you should notify any other recruiters from whom you have received offers that you have accepted another offer.

If you do not have a written offer, you may want to wait until you complete your first day of work before notifying other recruiters that you are no longer available. If you have an offer but believe that you will receive a better offer, your circumstances will dictate whether you take the "bird in the hand" or delay responding to the initial offer as long as reasonable.

Alternatively, you may decide to reject the offer in the hope that your belief is accurate. Hopefully, your belief is correct.

**TIP 6-83 Negotiate your compensation package strategically.**

The objective is to get as much money in your base pay or hourly rate as possible. If a sign-on bonus is offered, politely ask that the bonus amount be added to your annual salary. Typically, sign-on bonuses are one-time payments made to new employees to induce them to join the company. If the answer is *no*, suggest that a percentage of the bonus be added to your salary.

The more money you can get in your base salary when you are hired, the better. Benefits such as life insurance are based in your annual salary. You will not see any portion of a one-time, sign-on bonus in subsequent years of employment. Your annual salary will consist of only your base pay unless you are eligible for a performance-based bonus.

Hourly workers should try to determine the pay range for the position and suggest that, based on your knowledge, skill and experience, a higher hourly rate is warranted. Of course, make sure that you have the training, certifications, and so on, you say you have.

# CHAPTER 7

# On the Job…Don't Get Shot by a Bullet Labeled "To Whom It May Concern"

*The key to unlocking my potential is within me. It is in the power of my thought, my vision, and my commitment.*

—Author unknown

*Robert is a brilliant financier who is highly regarded in the business community. He makes time to mentor executives, those who aspire to be executives, and those in between.*

*A company that Robert knew intimately was undergoing a turbulent reorganization and cultural change. Several of the company's employees were Robert's friends, and they asked him to have lunch with them to discuss business developments and their thoughts on what some of the changes would be.*

*During lunch, Robert very smoothly leaned across the table, ran his gaze across each person's face, and told them to "do your job, mind your business, and keep your head down. It would be a shame for any of you to stick up your head and get shot by a bullet labeled 'to whom it may concern.'"*

*At first, Robert's friends did not understand. They all were solid performers with (they thought) reasonably secure jobs. Then it dawned on one of them what Robert was telling them: While they might not be on a layoff list, that could change at any time, for any reason. That is why he was telling them not to draw attention to themselves and to stay under the radar. When they finally "got it," they realized that their jobs could be at risk.*

*While they stayed under the radar, they considered their options. Some of them chose to stay with the company while one chose to accept another employment opportunity. Of those who chose to remain with the company, only one person regretted his decision.*

*Robert's friends learned invaluable lessons. First, no matter how well you perform or think you perform, job security is an oxymoron—a contradiction in terms. Most jobs are not secure.*

*Second, do not take anything for granted. For reasons unknown to you, and over which you have no control, your employment situation can change in the blink of an eye. You can change from hero to zero or, as one supervisor put it, from sugar to sh\*t, in a New York minute.*

*This is another reason to save money when you are employed.*

### TIP 7-84 Your success on the job depends on you.

You have the job. What is next? Learn your job. Learn your employer's business. After three to six months, venture out to meet people in other departments. Learn what they do.

Is your career goal to become a leader? To quote a line from *Hamilton*, do you want to be "in the room where it happens?" Do you want a seat at the table? "How to Get Noticed by Your Boss's Boss" identifies the 10 steps to take to place you on the radar screens of senior leaders.[1]

Some people rise to the top and some do not.[2] Two tips to help you rise include:

- Values: Establish core values.
  - Live by them.
  - Always maintain your integrity.
- Do not expect life to be fair.[3]

### TIP 7-85 Be the best employee you can be.

### TIP 7-86 Take advantage of opportunities to discuss the company with more senior employees.

---

[1] Raffoni, M. 2019. "How to Get Noticed by Your Boss's Boss." *Harvard Business Review,* October 14, 2019, https://hbr.org/2019/10/how-to-get-noticed-by-your-bosss-boss

[2] Abrams, R. 2020. "Your Employment Matters with Beverly Williams Podcast." *Learning to Rise in Your Career,* 2020, https://youremploymentmatters.com/podcast/

[3] Ibid.

**TIP 7-87 Step outside your comfort zone.**

Once again, unless you have an employment agreement or a legally enforceable employee handbook provision, or you are employed under a collective bargaining agreement or some other legally protected basis, you are or will be an employee at will.

This means that your employer (absent reasons prohibited by law) can discharge you at any time with or without just cause. Do not give your employer an excuse to do so. Fortunately for you, it is a two-way street.

You have a similar right. You can resign with or without prior notice. Remember: No one is irreplaceable. Furthermore, you should not resign without giving your employer a two-week notice unless there are extenuating circumstances.

Whatever you may think, your employment-related success will depend on you and only you.

- Once hired, aim to be the best employee you can be.
- Do not repeat mistakes; learn from them.
- Leave the attitude and excuses at home.
- Other people and events will affect you, but you will determine the extent to which you are affected.

You will make decisions that affect how you will be treated, regarded, compensated, and promoted. If you treat your supervisor or coworkers disrespectfully, you will not only be unsuccessful, you will not have your job for long.

Your mission is to establish yourself as an excellent performer with whom people enjoy working because of your positive attitude and the value you add to the team and the project.

- Do not frown, grouse, or make sarcastic comments.
- Continue to rely on etiquette books (e.g., *Emily Post's Etiquette, 18th ed., Gentle Manners, How to Be a Gentleman, How to Be a Lady, As a Gentleman Would Say*, and *As a Lady Would Say*) as reference sources.
- Practice workplace civility.

Perhaps you will be invited to attend a business luncheon with a client or to your boss's home for a social gathering. You may need the information in these books. If you are polite, considerate, and pleasant to work with, and if you produce a superior work product, you should do well.

If you are not successful at work, despite the previous list of attributes, you can decide that you have had enough, and look for another job. When you find one, resign.

**TIP 7-88 Become your own HR person.**
Never rely on anyone else to handle matters that are important to you. There may come a time when you have to prove that you were employed. Over time and with changes in leadership and supervision, information and documents can be lost and misplaced.

You should retain and maintain employment records, including offer letters, fringe benefit documents, salary and tax documents, performance reviews, and records of disciplinary action such as performance improvement plans and warnings. Be sure to include memoranda that memorialize discussions that took place whether or not disciplinary action was taken.

Save everything in two places and on cloud storage. Two flash drives or one flash drive and hard copies are options. Whichever option you select, place each one in a different albeit safe fireproof container and place.

Again, it is better to have and not need than to need and not have.

**TIP 7-89 Authority is not always handled well by everyone who has it.**
Look for employment with companies with an ethics program that applies to all employees regardless of level and includes, among other things,

- Ethical standards
- Policies and procedures that clearly set forth
  ○ What is expected of employees, and
  ○ The consequences for failure to comply
- Training
- Protections for employees who complain of unethical conduct based on a reasonable belief that wrongdoing has occurred
- Examples of unethical workplace behavior
  ○ Lying, stealing, cheating
  ○ Falsifying time reports

- Taking credit for work you did not do
- Making business decisions to benefit yourself or someone you know for financial gain
- Accepting bribes or kickbacks
- Disclosing trade secrets and other confidential information

You should know what your employer's policies are and comply with them.

**TIP 7-90 Do not sign anything until you read and understand what you are signing.**

**TIP 7-91 Respect authority and the chain of command.**

**TIP 7-92 When possible, even at work, continue to avoid toxic people.**

## Workplace Civility

Again, regardless of how you view yourself, it is important that "respect" be your touchstone in the employment environment and elsewhere. Hopefully, you have made it a permanent element of your personal brand.

Respect for yourself, others, and the company or business for which you work or want to work are prerequisites for success in the workplace.

- Speak to people in a respectful tone
- Require the same in return.
- Do not let your ego make you think you are better than others.

Conduct yourself in a manner that reflects your personal regard for yourself and others.

**TIP 7-93 Do not let anyone diminish your self-esteem.**
If you have never been told that you are special or been made to feel that you are, then begin by embracing the truth that you are not better than anyone else and no one is better than you are. As stated earlier, you may receive negative feedback about your performance and your promotion

prospects. If you do, consider all feedback a gift and accept it graciously. You should accept it, but you should not let it make you feel inferior.

Without regard to your race, gender, age, religion, gender expression, disability, ethnicity, or national origin, circumstances may cause you to develop a feeling of inferiority in a work environment, if you allow it. Bullies come in all races, genders, religions, and ages—and even adults and supervisors can be bullies.

Do not let anyone intimidate or bully you. Do not let anyone get into your head, so that you feel inferior or intimidated. If you experience bullying, speak to a mentor (if you have one) for advice or HR.

A mentor is someone whose judgment and professionalism you respect and whose knowledge of work situations may be helpful to you. You may find that you need more than one mentor. A respected higher-level employee, who knows your employer's culture and leaders is as important as the person whose judgment and professionalism you respect and rely on in making career decisions.

**TIP 7-94 Continue to research your employer after you are hired.**

**TIP 7-95 Look for creative ways to position yourself, so that your potential is recognized.**
Locate the research you conducted about your new employer in preparation for your job interviews. This material should become part of a research file that you maintain. Continue to search the Internet regularly and update your file as needed.

- Check the company's website for information.
- Read company-generated material to shareholders, the media, and professional organizations about business strategies.
- Attend evening meetings of relevant professional organizations.
- Visit professional organization websites to obtain material about topics discussed at meetings.

You do not have to spend money on subscriptions. Go to the library to read relevant business and trade publications to keep abreast of what is going on in your industry. The better informed you are, the better you will be able to discuss your employer's business and to ask appropriate, intelligent questions.

The information you gather, the discussions you initiate, and the questions you ask will help you engage in self-promotion.

- Volunteer for assignments and initiatives that have a companywide reach.
- Volunteer for company events that may be related to charities.

You will meet new people at your company. Show that you are a generous person, who is willing to help in any situation. Your objective is to work hard, produce exceptional results, and be so personable that you get yourself on the radar screen of influential company decision makers, managers, and administrative personnel.

**TIP 7-96 Learn your employer's abbreviations, language, and business culture.**

Employers use abbreviations and other shortcuts and shorthand to communicate with coworkers. You need to learn:

- The shortcuts and shorthand your employer uses
- What they mean
- How to use them appropriately

Your employer may have companywide initiatives with which you should also be familiar. For example, concepts (e.g., emotional intelligence and critical thinking) and tests and assessment tools (e.g., the Myers-Briggs Type Indicator) may be used by your company to improve worker productivity and effectiveness.

The Internet provides a wealth of information about these tools. It is to your benefit to become familiar with them.

**TIP 7-97 If you pay attention, people will show their true colors. When they do, reassess your opinion of and your relationship with them; you may regret it if you do not.**
People are not always as they seem. Not everyone is a good judge of character nor does everyone have sound judgment.

If discerning situations and people is not your strong suit, you have to find a method of identifying people who are untrustworthy, schemers, or scammers. These are people who mean you no good; moreover, no good will come from you letting this kind of individual get close to you.

It is also helpful to identify liars, cheats, "frenemies," and unethical characters. Ask yourself:

- "Would a friend or supporter behave toward me as this person does?"
- "Have I witnessed a person taking credit for work that I know he or she did not do?"
- "Have I heard some of my coworkers say things that are simply untrue?"

Some management types—as well as coworkers—may fall into these categories. It is important to protect yourself from these dangerous coworkers by creating a paper trail of e-mails, notes, memos, and letters to support your recollection of events.

You should realize, however, that you may not be able to avoid such a person, particularly if he or she is your supervisor. One possible approach is to get a mentor to help you strategize about how to handle such people.

*A good manager is a man who isn't worried about his own career but rather the careers of those who work for him.*
—H. S. M. Burns (1900 to 1971),
British president of Shell Oil Company

**TIP 7-98 Make your supervisor look good.**

**TIP 7-99 Do not try to teach your supervisor that you have a better style; it usually does not work.**

**TIP 7-100 If you have one approach and your supervisor has another, if persuasion fails, adopt your supervisor's approach.**

You do not have to be on the job long to understand that the workplace is not all about you. It is, however, mostly about your supervisor. In addition to delivering the best job performance, your primary objective is to make your supervisor's job easier and help him or her (and you) look good.

For example:

- Avoid asking your boss a lot of questions; instead, try to get your questions answered elsewhere.
- Anticipate every possible question your boss or others may ask about your presentation or project and be prepared to answer them.
- Always have a solution to challenges when you present them.
- Do not say things like, "They did not call/e-mail me back, so I do not know." Present the situation, but then offer a solution. Otherwise, you appear helpless and unable to think for yourself.
- If you are scheduled to meet with your supervisor:
  - Call to make sure he or she is on schedule.
  - Ask when your meeting should end, so that your supervisor does not fall further behind.
  - Be prepared for a meeting by reviewing any documents that may be necessary and have the material fresh in your mind.
  - Understand what your boss expects from you and what you bring to the table.
  - Push back or disagree with your supervisor and others tactfully.
- Being resourceful makes you valuable.
- Based on meetings and discussions, you may be able to anticipate what your supervisor will need from you before it is requested.
- Be sure to ask before beginning the work to confirm that you are correct and should proceed.

- Deliver outstanding results that exceed your supervisor's expectations.
- Volunteer to represent your group on company initiatives and committees, so that your boss does not have to spend time on these tasks. If possible, select the initiative or committee that has the most influential sponsors.

When you and your supervisor meet to discuss your project or any other topic, set forth your opinion or position concisely, in an organized fashion, and articulately. Coworkers may share their opinions on the project or topic but, in the end, go with your gut—even if it was not the popular choice. Just be sure that you have a sound basis for your position and be able to defend it.

You have an especially good chance of being successful if:

- You are a reliable, competent, hard-working person.
- You are pleasant to work with.
- You "think outside the box" or can learn to think that way.
- A creative approach to problem solving is part of your DNA.

You should:
- Remain informed about the business.
- Be courteous and pleasant.
- Leave your ego and attitude at home but bring your pride and self-esteem to work.
- Arrive ready to work on the days you are scheduled to work, which may mean arriving early to get breakfast out of the way regardless of what other employees do.
- Be accountable for your performance and your conduct.
- Identify what sets you apart from other employees (e.g., technological skills, writing skills, public speaking, and research) and improve those skills.
- Have a "can-do/will do" attitude.
- Follow through and follow up.
- Do not:
  - Be a clock-watcher
  - Be late to meetings

- ○ Text during meetings
- ○ Miss appointments

**Do not get it twisted:** If, after hearing your opinion, your supervisor disagrees and you push back tactfully, but he or she decides to pursue another course of action, then tactfully adopt the company line and be a productive team member. Learn when the discussion and debate are over.

Telltale signs include the following:

- Body language (arms folded, or the person stands up)
- Facial expressions
- Words or phrases like "I'm done," "I have heard enough," and "Enough"

### TIP 7-101 Do not overcommit and underdeliver.

It is crucial to meet deadlines; however, if you feel that you cannot meet a deadline:

- Notify your manager in advance or as soon as you realize it.
- Update him or her on the status of the project.
- Identify the challenges that prevent you from meeting your deadline.

One form of professional suicide occurs if you tell your boss that you will complete a task, assignment, or project by a certain date, and you do not deliver. You may get away with it once, but you might not be given future opportunities to disappoint the person who completes your performance review and determines how much of a salary increase you may receive.

It does not matter whether he or she asks you when you can complete the task or whether they give you the date by which it must be completed. It also does not matter if you have a good reason for not delivering as requested.

Rest assured: Your boss may not risk looking bad by giving you another chance.

- You must deliver!
- Reliability is essential.
- Excuses are unacceptable.

Except in very extreme circumstances, such as a close loved one becomes critically ill and is hospitalized or suddenly passes on, you simply need to honor your commitment. Deadlines must be met.

The quality of the completed assignment is equally important. If you wait until the last minute to begin the assignment, you will be sorry. Life continually interferes with work. To avoid any mishaps, begin immediately and be thorough. If appropriate, have someone else (with proofreading skills) check the finished product.

**TIP 7-102 Do not presume that you are performing well if you have not been told so, and your performance reviews do not confirm that you are.**

Generally, employers are not legally required to give employees performance reviews. There might be an exception where there is a company policy or a union-contract provision that creates an obligation.

Pride and ego should never interfere with your ability to be successful in the workplace nor should you rely on your high opinion of yourself to evaluate how well you are performing. Often, employees believe that they are stellar performers without their supervisor's formal input (or in spite of it).

**Ask for feedback:** If your supervisor has not provided feedback about your performance, do not take it for granted that he or she thinks you are doing a great job. Consider making an appointment to meet with your supervisor to discuss your performance and what you can do to improve.

Even if you are an excellent performer, there is always room for improvement. If you have a problem with your supervisor or a coworker, assume good intentions unless and until you confirm that your assumption is incorrect.

A distinguished professor advised his students, "When you hear hoofbeats in the hallway, think horses, not zebras."[4] In other words, the most common explanation is usually the correct one.

---

[4] Popik, B. 2010. Posted by, "When you Hear Hoofbeats, Think of Horses, not Zebras." Blog, *The Big Apple,* September 12, 2010, https://barrypopik.com/index.php/new_york_city/entry/when_you_hear_hoofbeats_think_of_horses_not_zebras

If you do not get along with your supervisor or coworkers, take a step back and a deep breath, and ask yourself if you are contributing to the problem. That is correct: *you.*

Ideally, you will receive constructive feedback about your performance prior to your annual performance review, so there will not be any surprises. If you find that you are not performing to your supervisor's satisfaction, do not immediately think that someone is out to get you or that you are the victim of illegal discrimination. It may be something more mundane.

The problem may be a breakdown in communications or a personality conflict, or you may not perform your job tasks in a manner that your supervisor finds acceptable. You may disagree, but if your supervisor is not happy with your performance, you will not be a happy employee.

Take time to consider whether there are simple answers to the problems you are having. Ask yourself:

- "Am I arriving to work on time and on the days I am scheduled to work?"
- "Are there issues with the quality of my work?"
- "Is my attitude an issue?"
- "Am I a team player?"

Of course, there are many more possibilities but, absent evidence to the contrary, nefarious, or illegal motives should be near the end of the list. There are supervisors, managers, and individuals at every level of management who are not effective leaders. They may be:

- Nice people, but weak or poor managers
- Unable to deliver negative feedback properly when it is needed
- Unable to exercise sound judgment
- People who are not so nice
- People who are incompetent

Yes. There are management types who are simply incompetent, outright liars. You will likely find that people who are incompetent are also unfamiliar with the truth.

There are also management bullies[5] in the workplace and coworkers who get a thrill out of making other employees feel small, making hurtful comments, and engaging in gossip. As any veteran or serviceperson will tell you, unfortunately you have to respect the position the person holds, even if you do not respect the person.

If you continue to work there:

- You must respect authority.
- You must also accept that your supervisor will remain in place until the right people find out the truth and do something about it.
- You also must accept that this may never happen.

You may be shocked to learn that people in higher positions are not always the best trained, the most knowledgeable, or, because of their conduct, the worthiest of respect or success. Again, the workplace is a microcosm of the world in which we live, with the attendant warts and blemishes. Try to avoid negative individuals who cannot say anything positive about anybody.

Likewise, do not be surprised to discover that those employed in higher positions are not better people either. They may have achieved more, and perhaps they are better educated or better trained, but they may still be unkind, unpleasant, and dishonest people.

Never forget that it is equally important that you be respected also. If you do not feel respected and valued where you work or apply for a job, look for employment elsewhere.

**Coworkers:** It is to your benefit to establish a reputation for being willing and able to help others, at work and elsewhere, as well as for reaching out to new people to make their transition into the organization easier.

## TIP 7-103 Cultivate a respectful relationship with coworkers at all levels in the organization and with clients.

## TIP 7-104 Help others reach their goals.

---

[5] Healthline. n.d. "How to Identify and Manage Workplace Bullying." Blog, *Healthline,* https://healthline.com/health/workplace-bullying

**TIP 7-105 Connect with new people in the organization.**

People active in their places of worship, charities, and civic and political organizations are likely to help or need help with projects and initiatives that may or may not advance their careers. Either way, it is a "win." The best way to move upward is to look for ways to connect with others to help them reach the level they want to achieve. You never know where that relationship might lead regarding future job opportunities.

You can offer to:

- Assist with preparing presentations.
- Proofread materials if you are a good proofreader.
- Write materials if you are a good writer.
- Be a sounding board.

It is important that, whatever you offer to do, do it well and on time. If you were asked, you would probably want someone to do the same for you. Think of it as a form of networking and good karma.

If one or more coworkers is a thorn in your side, again ask yourself whether you may somehow be contributing to the problem. You cannot change their behavior, but you can change your own behavior and how you respond to external events.

**TIP 7-106 Provide constructive criticism in a way that will make people seek your input.**

**TIP 7-107 Feedback should be given in a tactful, diplomatic manner.**

How to receive feedback or input (also known as "criticism") has been addressed. Giving feedback can be just as tricky as receiving it. Generally, feedback—especially constructive feedback—is expected, even encouraged. The trick is to deliver feedback in a manner that does not offend or anger the recipient. Always begin with positive feedback, such as things you liked:

- "I like the way you zeroed in on the issue."
- "Your presentation was crisp and focused on the critical issues."
- "You had a tough topic but explained it so simply. I understood everything, except ..."

- "Everyone was riveted by your presentation. It was so informative."

When you have exhausted the positive aspects, move on to the negative aspects of the presentation. One approach is to ask a question:

- "Do you think that the approach in your presentation addresses all of the options?"
- "I thought of an additional option. Do you think that this will work?"
- "We discussed another option last week, but I did not see it in the presentation. "Do you think it's still a viable option that should be included?"

If you master the talent of delivering constructive feedback and offer helpful suggestions, your opinion will become highly regarded, and your peers will ask for your help. The relationships you cultivate with employees at all levels should result in more requests for your input.

### TIP 7-108 Find a knowledgeable mentor and/or hire a career coach.

*Don't wait for someone to take you under their wing. Find a good wing and climb up underneath it.*
　　　　　　　　—Frank C. Bucaro, business motivational speaker

You will need experience and objectivity to help you navigate business cultures and deal with different personalities. After you have been on the job for at least a year (or sooner, if the need arises), you should identify a knowledgeable, senior employee and ask him or her to be your mentor.

Depending on your career aspirations, and if you are financially able, you may also want to retain a career coach. One person is familiar with the company; the other should be experienced in guiding professionals through their careers.

*An executive at a Fortune 500 company hired a career/executive coach for his son when he was only a senior in high school. The executive said that he wanted to make sure his son did not make any wrong turns as he moved through college, graduate, or professional school and beyond.*

**TIP 7-109 As a new hire, do not share your personal business in the workplace.**

Whether you are unemployed or employed, keep your own counsel, particularly about the details of your personal life. For example, your coworkers do not need to know that your loved one is in rehab or is about to be deported. Similarly, should you share information about the uncertain parentage of your children also known as "baby daddy dramas" and "baby mama dramas?"

Regardless of whether they should or should not, people make judgments about others based on, among other things, their personal biases, their upbringing, and their experiences. To be sure that you as an employee are judged on relevant factors (e.g., the quality of your work, your ability to work effectively as a member of a team, and your attention to detail), remember to keep your personal and family life at home.

If you are responsible for a loved one, have back-up childcare or eldercare arrangements in place. This is your personal business. Your problems are not your employer's problems.

This is especially true when many people are unemployed, and you can easily be replaced. After you have worked for a year or more, you may be eligible for job-protected family leave, if you need it. If you find that you cannot handle your personal situation on your own, before you speak to anyone at work, conduct research to determine whether you meet the requirements for job-protected leave.

**Do not get it twisted:** Please do not misunderstand. This advice is neither to avoid making friends at work nor to be embarrassed by the conduct or life situations of your loved ones. This advice is not based on making judgments but on recognizing that judgments may be made about you without your knowledge.

Rather, be mindful not to give anyone ammunition that can potentially derail and adversely affect your career. Many rewarding relationships originate in the workplace, but not all of them stand the test of time. "Friend" coworkers cautiously.

*A group of young women, who were about to graduate from an administrative-assistant program, were sent on interviews to obtain employment. The program's instructors were sure that the young woman who had received the highest grades and typed the fastest and most accurately would be the first student hired. She was considered an especially attractive candidate because, in addition to her skills, she had a pleasant personality and demeanor.*

*Within two weeks, everyone except the top performer had received an offer of employment. The instructors could not understand it. One of them asked the young woman to describe her interview, particularly the questions she was asked and her responses to them.*

*According to the young woman, the interviewer asked her, "What would it mean to you if you were offered the job?" The young woman answered, "It would mean that I could bring my young son to live with me. Right now, he lives with my grandmother in Massachusetts."*

The instructors could not be sure, but they had their suspicions. They believed that the reason the young woman did not receive an offer, at least from that employer, was because she may have unwittingly revealed (or the interviewer concluded) that she was an unwed mother or otherwise ensnared in drama.

**Remember:** People prejudge others based on, among other things, their upbringing, biases, limited education, personal experiences, or knowledge.

### TIP 7-110 Keep your loved ones out of the workplace.

"The 'Millennials' Are Coming" is a provocative look at Generation Y (also known as Millennials or young people born between 1980 and 1995). According to this *60 Minutes* segment, many Millennials are reared and educated in a supervised, monitored, coached environment and are not prepared for the "cold realities of work."[6] If this is true, well-meaning helicopter parents have a nickel in that dime.

The segment recounts how a particularly interested parent contacted her child's supervisor to challenge the performance report her child had received. Take the time to view the segment on the *60 Minutes* site or locate it on the Internet. You may find it entertaining as well as instructive about the perceptions related to Millennials.

Admittedly, Millennials are not the only segment of the population that allows their loved ones to insinuate themselves into the workplace.

---

[6] 60 Minutes, CBS-TV, "The 'Millennials' Are Coming, Morley Safer on The New Generation of American Workers." May 25, 2007, https://cbsnews.com/news/the-millennials-are-coming/

The well-meaning spouses and significant others of each generation have also been known to intrude inappropriately into the workplace. The parents of Millennials, however, are persistent.

You should almost never have someone else call your employer on your behalf. The only exception may be if you are too sick to inform your supervisor that you will be absent.

*Greta wanted to take vacation time during the week her husband's plant was closed. Unfortunately, another employee had requested the same time off and received approval before Greta made her request.*

*The size of the staff and the workload required that Greta remain on the job. Rather than accept that she could not take off the time, Greta let her husband call her supervisor to persuade him to grant her vacation request. The supervisor appropriately refused to speak to Greta's husband about the matter.*

Issues of privacy preclude your employer from discussing (or disclosing) most matters with anyone but you. Furthermore, your supervisor's opinion of you may be diminished by such behavior.

### TIP 7-111 Do not engage in criminal, unethical, or otherwise unprofessional behavior on or off the job.

You would be surprised by the number of people who smoke marijuana during working hours and on company property. Consumption of alcohol at lunch (while not illegal) occurs and is also ill-advised.

Work-related social activities should always be considered work, especially if management is in attendance. It seems obvious that social drinking at work-related events should be kept to a minimum. You will be invited to events where alcohol is served. Even if your boss or others get drunk, do not join that group! Too many embarrassing things happen at holiday parties and happy hours. You do not want to be the one everyone is talking about the next morning.

- Pace yourself.
- Have a drink, but then grab a glass of water to remain hydrated.
- Consume your drink slowly.
- Do not drink at all or have a nonalcoholic beverage that looks like a cocktail.

You want to be in control of yourself at all times and present a favorable impression about your judgment and professionalism. Anything less may be held against you. It is simply risky to have too much of a good time with friends who work with you.

### TIP 7-112 At work, the only place you should expect privacy is behind the locked door of a bathroom stall.

Whether you work in an open-spaced environment, one with cubicles, a combination of the two, your own office, or another configuration entirely, there is little privacy in the workplace. At work, it is wise to conduct yourself professionally, especially when interacting with a client.

Keep in mind that those around you can hear you. If you want to gossip or talk about personal things, do not do it at your desk. Wait until you leave. The walls of enclosed offices and conference rooms can be quite thin.

Even if you think that no one can hear you, it is never a certainty. Moreover, it looks unprofessional and immature to see a person whispering. This is not high school.

Once you get a job, do not engage in behavior that will cause you to lose it.

- Keep in mind that your employer owns the telephones, computers, and just about everything else you use at work.
- Do not expect privacy on any electronic device provided by your employer.
- It is common for employers to have policies that prohibit or limit employees's personal use of company hardware and software.
- Do not visit controversial websites that are not work related.
- Do not use your computer for personal business, including doing schoolwork, conducting personal research, paying bills, or logging onto your personal e-mail account from work.
- Pornography sites should never be accessed at work.
- It is not unusual for employers to monitor their employees's system use.
- It is better to be safe than sorry.

**TIP 7-113 Continue to conduct periodic self-assessments.**

After you have been on the job for a while, take time to look in the mirror and determine whether you like what you see. Are you an honest, hard-working person of integrity of whom your loved ones can be proud? If you are not, you should regroup and make the necessary changes to put you on the right path.

You also want to stay on track with your career plan and your personal brand, which includes checking your e-mail regularly and answering your phone after you are hired. If you do not check your e-mail, you may not have the most current information from your supervisor.

Admittedly, you may not have information because your job or your level in the company does not warrant it. Remember: No one has all the information about everything or any one thing. You may not know why the information is not available to you, or it may be available but only some of it.

In the workplace, as in the military, much information is disclosed only on a need-to-know basis. Your employer may be trying to sell the company, and you do not know it.

The office grapevine may seem like a reliable source of information, but do not be fooled. It would be a serious error in judgment to rely on the office grapevine and then repeat what you hear. It would also be foolhardy to ignore it completely.

Gossip, by definition, is unreliable. Nonetheless, there may be a kernel of truth to the stories circulating throughout the office. Do not gossip or rely on it, but do not dismiss it. You may not know what is true and what is conjecture or pure fabrication. File gossip away in your memory but only use it after careful and judicious analysis and deliberation.

**TIP 7-114 Loyalty and trust are important but not always reciprocated.**

- Companies are not loyal, but individuals should be.
- Be loyal to your employer and your supervisor.
- If you cannot be loyal to your current employer, you should look for another job.
- Do not make mistakes that will require your supervisor to defend you to more senior employees. Your supervisor may not do so.

- If you decide to be loyal to other individuals, make sure they deserve it and are loyal to you.
- Do not "throw anyone under the bus" unless there are legal implications, or you are asked a direct question that requires a direct, honest answer.
- Take responsibility for your actions and be honest if you mess up. Even if reprimanded, you will learn from the experience.
- It helps to have a friend at work, preferably in another department, to expand your network and expose yourself to different points of view.

If, after you are hired, you do not believe that your employer operates in accordance with the values that attracted you in the first place, do not quit your job until you find employment elsewhere. Your professional and personal reputation is your stock in trade. You do not want to be tainted professionally because you work for a company exposed on the front pages of national news outlets as one that engages in criminal or otherwise unethical activities.

## Network, Network, Network ...

After you become employed, maintain the contacts you made and the network you developed during your job search. You never know when you may need them again.

The journey that ends with acquiring a new position typically includes meeting and otherwise interacting with people whom you knew previously and those whom you met along the way.

It is wise to maintain and update your network database regularly. Even if you never need them again for a job search, you may need to reach out to the contacts in your network for support for community, environmental, and charitable efforts.

**Remember:** It is better to have and not need than to need and not have.

**TIP 7-115 If you cannot take it anymore, find another job before you resign.**[7]

---

[7] Thanks to Adrienne Colotti for her substantial contribution to this section.

It is not unusual to go through "ruts" and to become unhappy with your job. This may be temporary, but it is important never to let it show when at work. Do not develop an attitude because you are unhappy.

Your problem is yours and should not be taken out on your coworkers and supervisor. If you are interviewing elsewhere, keep it to yourself.

- Do not share with people at work because it will get around.
- If you are miserable, do not try to make everyone else miserable, too.

*According to Bella, who is under 35 and has managed several teams that include young professionals, they are shy and reluctant to reach out to executives to ask questions or to obtain needed information. The reason young professionals give for their hesitancy is that they do not know the executive, or they do not want to bother him or her. (Remember Dorly's story from Chapter 2.)*

*Bella says,*

*I tell them, 'That is your fault. You need to get up and be assertive and introduce yourself. These are not mean or intimidating people.*

*You are letting their title scare you, and they are very friendly and easy to talk to. To me, it is not an excuse to say that you do not know them when it is your job to know them.'*

*'You cannot expect to be walked around, handheld, and introduced to every single person when you're new to a company. At some point, you have to take control and get to know who you need to know in order to do your job well.'*

Before you decide to resign, consider the following:

- Do not make decisions about your career when you are emotional. Give yourself time to calm down and think about the situation when you are calm. Sometimes people become frustrated with their bosses, certain projects, or coworkers, and get worked up and decide to quit. Wise decisions are rarely made in such circumstances.

- It is important to be able to handle change and transition in the workplace. Turnover is common and transitions happen often. It is important to "go with the flow" and not get caught up in it. People prefer to remain in their comfort zones at work. When leadership at an executive level changes, there may be significant changes that affect your job. Do not panic! Be patient during these times and remind yourself that it is temporary. In a few months, you will look back and realize that you were able to adjust (hopefully).
- Can you afford to quit your job until you find another one? How long did it take you to find the job you have? Have you saved enough money to support yourself for at least a year?
- Do not resign unless you mean it.
- If you decide to quit your job:
  - Never burn bridges. It is a cliché but so true.
  - Depart professionally.
  - Do not decide to tell anyone what you think of them.
  - Give your employer at least a two-week notice.
  - Be flexible.
  - Offer to stay to transition someone, if needed. It shows that:
    1. You care about your team's success; and
    2. You do not want to ditch them and leave them to figure out projects that you owned.

*Barbara, who has been employed in different areas of the advertising industry since college, and each time left one company for a better opportunity, offers the following advice:*

*"I cannot tell you how many times I run into someone I knew in another job … people always resurface, and it is good when they recall you in a positive way."*

*"Someone you dislike on your team could become your client one day for all you know … people jump around a lot in careers and you never know where you or they will end up."*

**Do not get it twisted:** Once again, do not quit your current job until you have another one.

No matter how well you perform or how much you deserve to be promoted, you cannot force an employer to promote you. Furthermore, despite what you may think, remaining on a job year after year does not entitle an employee to a promotion. You have other options.

Look for another job, and do your "due diligence," or homework, about the companies you plan to contact for employment opportunities. Keep the job you have but plan your departure.

Make yourself more marketable so that, when the job market improves, you are positioned to move into a job (perhaps with another employer) where there is more opportunity to advance.

Take advantage of tuition-assistance programs to obtain a higher degree or additional training. Before spending money on online degrees, research the educational institution. Ask HR professionals and business contacts what they think of the institution. Check with your mentor if you have one. Confirm that an online degree is the most cost-effective or respected path to an advanced degree. Be sure that the monetary investment you plan to make will yield the benefits you desire.

- Take additional training courses to acquire more skills and obtain certifications.
- Get involved in charitable, civic, community, and professional organizations to increase your networking contacts.
- Do not be afraid to "move on to move up" because you cannot rely on the job-security concept of yesterday.

"We spend most of our days at work; it is therefore very important that we get along with our employers, employees, colleagues, and clients."[8]

**Human resources:** Traditionally, HR is the department responsible for recruiting, hiring, onboarding new hires, assessing talent, training, administering payroll and employee benefits, and disciplining and discharging employees.

Depending on the employer's size, organizational structure, and culture, HR may also be responsible for organizational leadership,

---

[8] "Employer-Employee-Relationships: How to relate to your employees/ your employer" http://relationship-affairs.com/Employer-Employee-Relationships.html

employment- and labor-law compliance, and mobility management, particularly as it applies to expatriates (i.e., U.S. citizens and foreign-born individuals, who work outside their countries either permanently or temporarily).

Your employer may have an HR policy and procedure manual or an employee handbook, which contains the company's rules, standards, and guidance about recruitment, compensation, benefits, training, and retention and termination of employment. Generally, there is no legal obligation to provide a policy manual or handbook, so some employers do, and some do not.

If, after you are hired, you are given an HR manual or employee handbook and are then requested to sign a document that acknowledges that you received the manual, read the document carefully so you know what you are signing. Likewise, read the manual or handbook because it may contain the procedural standards and workplace rules to which you will be held as an employee. In some states, an employee handbook is considered an employment contract. Thus, you may have rights that you did not know about, but your employer also has rights.

*Erica started a new job right after college. Within six months, she knew the company was not a good fit for her. Erica discretely began a new job search.*

*Less than a year after her start date, she resigned because she had found a job she believed she would like better than the job she had.*

*She took a two-week vacation and began her new job when she returned. After working for three days she was served with a complaint. She was being sued by her former employer.*

*Erica had signed a noncompete agreement. Her former employer alleged that Erica's new employer was their competitor and that Erica had violated her noncompete agreement.*

*Erica had several sleepless nights, lawyers got involved but the matter was resolved without a trial. Fortunately for Erica, her aunt's friend was an attorney.*

### A Few Things You Should Know

Whether or not you have had a job before, you may not know that employees and employers have rights and that employee benefits can be advantageous and save you money.

Employers' rights are:

- Identified in employment contracts, including (where applicable) policy manuals and employee handbooks, and collective bargaining agreements (union contracts);
- Implied by law; and
- Imposed by federal and state law.

Employers have a right to:

- Rely on employees's representations about skills and experience;
- Require certain performance levels from employees;
- Direct the work to be performed;
- Expect that employees do not reveal trade secrets or confidential information; and
- Expect that employees will work exclusively for the employer during the workday.

The obligations between employers and employees are generally regulated by legislation and case law.

Employees must:

- Be paid for work done;
- Receive equitable compensation (i.e., same classification, same skills = similar wages);
- Be compensated in accordance with the appropriate collective bargaining agreement, if applicable; and
- Receive the same fringe benefits as others in their job classification.

Employers must provide:

- A reasonably safe workplace; and
- Accurate personnel records.

HR can be helpful as you learn your way around the company and learn how things are done. Remember, however, that:

- HR works for your employer and, as such, owes a duty to your mutual employer to act in the employer's best interest.
- Ideally, your interest and your employer's interest will be aligned, but that may not always be true.
- As with any staff, all HR employees are not created equal; some have more experience and knowledge than others.

Employee relations is a discipline within the HR function of a nonunion business or a business that has both union and nonunion employees, and which typically handles:

- Compensation and benefits
- Workplace safety
- Recruitment, selection, and talent management
- Performance management
- Discipline and discharge

Employee relations specialists identify and resolve workplace issues concerning allegations of discriminatory employment practices, including sexual and otherwise unlawful harassment.

They may also conduct or assist with workplace investigations and address:

- Employer responses to nonunion employee complaints
- Employee engagement and satisfaction
- Turnover and retention issues
- Management of performance-related issues
- Management of employee recognition initiatives
- Representation of the employer at unemployment hearings, interactions between employers, employees, and unions or other organizations that represent those employees.
  - ○ **Open shop**—This is a business in which union and non-union workers are employed and in which union membership is not a condition of securing or maintaining employment.

- *Closed shop*—This is a workplace in which the employer has agreed to employ only members of a particular labor union. Employees must remain members of the union to remain employed.
- *Agency shop*—This requires that every company employee who works in a position that is in the union's bargaining unit must pay the union an amount equal to the union's customary initiation fees and monthly dues or a percentage thereof. An agency shop does not require that an employee:
  1. Become an official union member.
  2. Become a union member before being hired.
  3. Take an oath or obligation or observe any internal union rules and regulations except the payment of dues or agency fee.

Labor relations specialists are typically responsible for matters involving labor-management issues, such as:

- Collective bargaining negotiations
- Grievances
- Arbitration
- Work stoppages/slowdowns
- Strikes

**TIP 7-116 Take advantage of your employer's benefits.**
If your employer has an employee assistance program, check it out. You may not need it now, but you may need it later.

**Employee benefits:** The array of fringe benefits available to employees varies from employer to employer. As soon as possible before or soon after you begin to work, review the benefits offered and take advantage of them. Many employers offer the following benefits and more.

**Tuition assistance or tuition reimbursement:** This is a benefit designed to assist employees who wish to attend college or university classes, so that they may expand their knowledge and skills.

Read tuition-assistance materials carefully because your employer may:

- Set a dollar limit available to each employee annually;
- Establish the number of classes they will pay for each year for each employee through tuition assistance;
- Require employees to pay for their own tuition and books when they register for classes;
- Reimburse the employee when he or she submits the receipts and evidence of earning a "C" or above grade upon completion of the class; and/or
- Require that the employee sign an agreement to pay back within a certain period of time the tuition assistance if he or she leaves the organization and substantial amounts are spent on tuition assistance.[9]

If tuition assistance is offered, and you do not have an undergraduate or a graduate degree, consider enrolling in courses or plan to do so the following year. Tuition-assistance programs are a cost-effective means of enhancing your skillset and marketability at your employer's expense.

Unless your employer has a policy that provides otherwise, accepting tuition assistance should not preclude you, subject to approval from your supervisor, from also enrolling in training programs offered by your employer on-site, online, or at another location. The objective is to obtain as much training at your employer's expense as possible.

**Employee assistance programs ("EAPs")** are an employee benefit provided by employers to assist employees and members of their households with personal issues that might negatively affect job performance. Short-term counseling and support may be all that an employee needs.

Generally, for longer-term counseling and support, a referral to another agency or provider is offered.

**EAPs:**

- Are frequently, although not always, offered in conjunction with the employer's health insurance plan; and

---

[9] Heathfield, S. 2019. "Employer-Sponsored Tuition-Assistance Options." Blog, *thebalancecareers,* Updated July 24, 2019, https://thebalancecareers.com/tuition-assistance-1918278

- May provide needs assessment, counseling, and referrals for employees and their family members when faced with mental health or emotional issues.

Typically, EAPs are available to assist the employee when he or she needs help dealing with life events, workplace issues, and other personal problems and challenges. For example, if an employee's spouse or child has a substance-abuse problem, the employee may contact the EAP to get help from professionals to deal with the issue in a private manner.[10]

According to the U.S. Department of Labor, EAPs most frequently assist employees in dealing with issues in the following areas:

- Alcoholism
- Drug abuse
- Marital difficulties
- Financial problems
- Emotional problems
- Legal issues

These programs typically offer a wide range of support for employees to help them obtain information about some of the following topics:

- Childcare or eldercare
- Short-term counseling for emotional and psychological issues
- Referral services related to situations, such as:
  - Job loss
  - Possible job loss
  - Long-term unemployment
  - Evictions and foreclosures that result in anxiety, depression, and hopelessness

If your employer offers an EAP, review the material to determine whether you can benefit from the services offered.

---

[10] U.S. Office of Personnel Management, Work-Life, Employee Assistance Programs, https://opm.gov/policy-data-oversight/worklife/employee-assistance-programs/

Do not be embarrassed! Tell your HR person that you are in crisis and you need help. Before you share sensitive information with your employer's EAP, confirm that the information will remain confidential.

**Employee stock option plans** are benefit plans that some employers offer their employees to enable them to acquire ownership in the company through the purchase of stock. Consult a qualified financial expert to plan your financial future. Save for a rainy day.

**Employee stock purchase plans** are another benefit offered by employers to give their employees the opportunity to buy stock in the company. The plan may be part of a qualified retirement plan, such as a 401(k), or it may simply be a benefit offered by the employer.

There are websites that provide basic information, but it is wise to consult a qualified financial expert.

**A 401(k) plan** is a deferred-compensation plan, which is established by an employer who pays for the administration of the plan. Qualified employees are allowed to authorize pretax payroll deductions and defer the taxes on the principal and earnings until retirement. Employers may elect to match employee contributions up to a specified amount.

Employee benefits often offer opportunities that can enhance your marketable skills and financial future. It is a mistake to overlook them.

## Resources

The unluckiest generation in U.S. history, Andrew Van Dam https://washingtonpost.com/business/2020/05/27/millennial-recession-covid/

16 Signs You Should Quit Your Job, Lynn Taylor https://psychologytoday.com/us/blog/tame-your-terrible-office-tyrant/201901/16-signs-you-should-quit-your-job

Signs It's Time to Quit Your Job, Alison Doyle https://thebalancecareers.com/signs-its-time-to-quit-your-job-2062292

16 signs it's time to quit your job, Rachel Gillett February 18, 2016 https://businessinsider.com/signs-you-should-quit-your-job-2016-2

Even if Your New Job is a Bad Fit, Don't Quit, Sue Shellenbarger, Wall Street Journal, Updated Jan. 2, 2018, https://wsj.com/articles/even-if-your-brand-new-job-is-a-bad-fit-dont-quit-1514906394

# CHAPTER 8

# Lights, Cameras, Action!

*I, not events, have the power to make me happy or unhappy. Today, I can choose which it shall be.*

—Groucho Marx (1890 to 1977),
American comedian, film, and television star

## Personal Considerations

**TIP 8-117 Think of the employment experience as a film production.** Each phase of your employment life will require that you project an image that translates into success. Depending on your personality and your life experience to date, achieving success may require stepping outside your comfort zone.

If you are shy, reticent, and soft spoken, you will need to call upon your inner being to help you project an image that differs from the person you are. If you are an extrovert with an exuberant, bubbly personality, you may have to dial back your personality.

The challenge is to strike a balance, which results in a persona that employment decision makers find appealing. Unfortunately, what constitutes a balance may change from interview to interview, and from employer to employer.

One way to think of your employment experience is to envision it as the production of a film.

- Always remember that the employer is the "money man" or the producer of the film.
- Never underestimate the power the producer has over the production.
- The director (at least over your performance) and an actor in the film, you, too, have power.

- Your objective as both actor and director is to give and get the best performance possible.
- As the director, you decide the role you will play: star, supporting actor, or extra.
- You are acutely aware that the producer may decide that you are well suited for roles in which you have no interest.
- The producer may also decide that you are not suited for bigger roles.
- Recognize that (1) there is an inherent bias or conflict of interest when "directors" evaluate their own performance; and (2) because you lack objectivity, your assessment of your performance may not be sound or reliable, especially if the producer's assessment is inconsistent with yours.
- If you do not feel that your contribution to the film is valued, or if you do not feel it is the right role for you, leave the film.
- Generally, you should not leave one role unless you are sure you have another one.
- You know or should know your circumstances better than anyone else.

The decision is yours.

**Do not get it twisted:** Stay grounded. The film production analogy is not an invitation for you to go "Hollywood." Diva-like behavior and thinking that you are the next Beyoncé or Lady Gaga, Leonardo DiCaprio, or Andy Cohen are not recommended.

It is your decision whether to remain in the role or leave when you have found another producer (employer), who appears to appreciate your talents and offers you a better opportunity. Your decision should not be made in the heat of anger or without well-reasoned reflection.

Checkout the film "The Intern" starring Ann Hathaway and Robert DeNiro. "The Intern" is a delightful story about a Millennial, a Baby Boomer, and their coworkers. They learned to work together for their mutual benefit, and ultimately for the benefit of Hathaway's business.

The development of the characters portrayed by Hathaway and DeNiro and the unexpected synergies that developed between them is a testament to the benefits of collaboration and working together. "The Intern" should become a staff development training film.

### TIP 8-118 Strike a balance between your work responsibilities and your home life.

Do not work to the exclusion of everything and everyone else. Success at work will enable you to be independent and enjoy some of the pleasures of life. If you work too many hours each day, every day, you will miss the pleasures and events that motivate you. Make sure to stop and smell the flowers.

**Do not get it twisted:** Do not tell your supervisor that you have worked enough for one week. If you are an hourly employee, there may be scheduled and unscheduled overtime. Salaried employees may work more hours without additional pay. When there are deadlines or unexpected situations that require you to work longer hours, do what is necessary.

### TIP 8-119 Give back by making charitable donations and/or donating your time.

Whatever good you do comes back to you. Giving of yourself and your time is rewarding on many levels. Do not forget those less fortunate because a change in circumstances could find you in their place. Remember to save for a rainy day.

**TIP 8-120 If life gives you lemons, make lemonade.**
Turn a negative into a positive.

**TIP 8-121 Be prepared to do the work necessary to achieve your goal.**
Most successful people who have achieved the career and life goals they set for themselves are usually willing to share with others what they learned along the way, especially those just beginning the journey.

- You understand that the journey will likely test your resilience and self-confidence.
- You should always remember that "you have the freedom to pull the superstar out of yourself"[1] to become the superstar you were born to be.
- You must be prepared to do the work to achieve success.

Consider a few life lessons from Shawn Carter, successful rapper and entrepreneur, better known as Jay-Z:

- Never fear the truth.
- The work you put in will be what you get out.
- Believe in and be true to yourself.
- Bring your best.
- Learn from your failures as well as your successes.
- Stand for something.
- Have integrity and honor.
- Master how to let go so you can move on.[2]

Learn more about the successful people you respect and want to emulate by reading whatever you can find about their climb to success, remembering always that success is defined differently by different people.

---

[1] Lady Gaga on "Mastering the Art of Fame." 60 Minutes, February 13, 2011. https://cbsnews.com/news/lady-gaga-on-mastering-the-art-of-fame-06-06-2011/3/
[2] "Oprah Presents Master Class with Jay-Z." https://worldstarhiphop.com/videos/video.php?v=wshheB4F9v7FJntwGtgf

Again, the Internet is a treasure trove of useful information. You can achieve your goals if you do the work, providing your goals are:

- Realistic
- Reasonable
- Attainable given your skillset, experience, education, personality, and work ethic

Remember the picture in the frame that you placed on your desk or by your bedside? Tell yourself, "I can do anything. I can achieve anything that I put my mind to if I work hard and meet the requirements identified." It is the truth.

Before you begin your employment journey, either to get hired or be promoted, be sure that you have done all the work necessary to move onward and upward. If you have, then lights, camera, action—it is time for you to star in your chosen career.

**TIP 8-122 Before you begin each day, remember that whether you will be happy is your choice.**

**TIP 8-123 Do not let anyone make that choice for you or steal your joy.**

> *No matter what your history has been, your destiny is what you create today. What are you going to create?*
> —Steve Maraboli, speaker, author,
> personal coach, and national radio show host

Rely on yourself to set your course and navigate the employment terrain. Do not expect your job search and subsequent success on the job to be a priority with anyone else, including your loved ones. It is not that they do not care or are not interested. They simply have their own concerns and interests.

Never be afraid to be your own cheerleader. There is nothing to be ashamed of if you set goals for yourself, create a plan, execute your plan, and take pride in your accomplishments. Once you achieve success as you define it, take time to enjoy it. You deserve it!

*Don't be afraid of the space between your dreams and reality. If you can dream it, you can make it so.*

—Belva Davis, television and radio journalist

### TIP 8-124 In the new, multi-employment reality… NAIL IT!

**Network** with people of all walks of life, cultures, nationalities, and beliefs to maximize the likelihood that favorable employment results will be achieved. Whether you are employed or unemployed, student, parent, or grandparent, be sure to utilize old-school and new-school networking methods.

Social media and "live" and virtual in-person networking should be used simultaneously and vigorously to achieve employment success. Do not network with only people who look and think as you do. Expand your network. It will surprise you.

**Accept feedback**, whatever the source, as the gift it is. You cannot afford to be thin-skinned. If you receive input from someone you do not agree with, ask yourself why you disagree. Hopefully, it is not because they are different.

Never dismiss feedback without consideration. Feedback, especially negative feedback, should be accepted graciously regardless of the recipient's race, gender, or generation. Although constructive feedback is helpful, negative feedback can also be useful.

**Also ask questions.** Be inquisitive. Do not be afraid to say you do not know but make the effort to find out before you do so.

**Improve** (whenever possible) your skillset, networking skills, communication skills.

**Learn** as much as you can about all that you can. One of the benefits of working in a "multi" environment is that there are so many opportunities to learn something new because everyone brings something unique to the discussion.

Remember, men and women of different ethnicities, national origins, and religions, regardless of their sexual and gender expression, or disabilities and abilities, all have something to share. Consider your coworkers and their differences as an instructional opportunity for you to learn about a variety of cultures, different ways of doing things, and multiple points of view.

Likewise, acknowledge the importance of the industry experience and institutional knowledge of employees with more years of service and work experience. If you have a degree, do not dismiss, or underestimate the contributions of individuals who may not have degrees.

Also enhance your skillset by acquiring additional training and education. Take advantage of free or low-cost offerings or, if you are employed, employer-compensated training and educational benefits. Improving written and oral communication skills is never a bad investment.

**Invest** your time, money, and energy in improving yourself and the world you live in wherever you live. Volunteer.

**Tenacity** is your friend. Whatever goals you set, if you put forth the effort, do not give up and do not accept rejection. View rejection as a form of feedback and use it to your advantage.

Time management is also important because there are only 24 hours in each day. To achieve employment success, as you define it, will take a commitment to and work on the task. Never let it consume you. Always take time to smell the roses or do something that makes you smile.

Embrace the new, multi-employment reality and learn from it.

*"Many of life's failures are people who did not realize how close they were to success when they gave up." —Thomas Edison, American inventor and businessman*

*"Nothing is impossible, the word itself says 'I'm possible'!" —Audrey Hepburn, British actress and humanitarian.*

**TIP 8-125 Learn to SOAR.**

# SOAR

A documentary film entitled *SOAR* explores the relationship between two sisters who also happen to be producers of the film. Kiera is a quadruple amputee who contracted pneumococcal sepsis and lost her limbs at age two. Uriah was born a month before her sister's illness.

The film explores several facets of the sisters's lives. It celebrates the extraordinary ways that Kiera has learned to adapt—as a dancer, choreographer, and medical assistant. It also explores Uriah's development as a dancer and choreographer and her decision to pursue a career in the building trades.

You read correctly. Kiera dances.

At the end of the documentary, it occurred to me that both Kiera and Uriah not only are developing multiple revenue streams, they are following their passions and interests.

*SOAR*, the documentary, and the letters S-O-A-R form the foundation of a strategy for navigating the ever-changing employment reality.

**S** stands for **Sharing** your skills and knowledge with coworkers and others and collaborating with them by networking with people of all walks of life, cultures, nationalities, and beliefs. If necessary, actively seek out these people, get to know them, and learn about their cultures and languages. Social media and "live" and virtual in-person networking should be used simultaneously and vigorously.

Do not just network with people who look and think as you do. If you work remotely, you will need to make a special effort to connect with friends, coworkers, and new people online and in-person. Face-to-face exchanges are helpful to sharpen verbal communication skills including establishing eye contact and body language.

In fact, when you look for a job, text, Snapchat, Instagram, and so on, do not forget the benefits of human contact and interactions. In this new-school, high-tech, electronic world, there is simply no substitute for old-school, "live," person-to-person contact. This method of networking, especially through referrals and recommendations, can almost magically get a person in the door for at least an exploratory or courtesy interview.

**S** also stands for **Seeking information** rather than affirmation. Family and friends are not objective about you and your talents. Input from an eclectic group of people you can rely on to give you constructive, objective feedback is not only important, it is essential.

If you can, find men and women of various ages, ethnicities, religions, and gender expressions, along with professionals employed in a multitude of functions who know you well enough to be helpful as you plan your career. If you cannot amass such a group, do the best you can with the people you know. Going forward, your efforts to expand your network base and make it as varied as possible will only help.

**O** stands for **O**perating throughout your life and career with integrity and dignity. In the workplace, you always want it said that you are a reliable, hard worker, who is creative and resourceful (in other words, goes beyond what which is expected).

You want to be considered trustworthy as well as a person of good character and integrity, who can be relied upon to tell the truth. As you go forward, your reputation should precede you, and it should be a reputation you can be proud of.

**O** also stands for **O**pening your mind to change, new ideas, and new people and keeping it open.

**A** stands for **A**cquiring information and knowledge. The information you obtain and the knowledge you acquire will improve your ability to stay abreast of your industry's developments and global influences and enhance your skillset.

Unbiased, reliable information is powerful and should be used wisely and judiciously. If nothing else, it enables you to make well-reasoned career and life decisions.

**A** also stands for **A**ssuming responsibility for your career and its development.

You will position yourself to be a sought-after candidate for any position you seek by:

- Proactively and strategically managing your employment journey;
- Making well-thought-out career decisions; and
- Refuting, by your conduct, negative, inaccurate perceptions about you and your generation, gender, and race.

Your personal brand or reputation includes your public and private behavior, what you say, how you say it, and how you present yourself. These things influence how you are perceived by others. Protect your personal brand. It evolves over time based on these perceptions and the opinions that result from them. A personal brand takes a long time to build and only moments to destroy.

**R**espect the rights of others. Your employment reality is "multi." It is multigenerational, multireligious, multinational, multiracial, multigender/

sexual expression and staffed with individuals with different perspectives and viewpoints.

You should not only accept, but respect that your coworkers may have different religions, nationalities and different abilities and disabilities. You may disagree with how they self-identify their race and gender. In your opinion, it may be more than questionable, it may be patently wrong. Your coworkers, not you, decide how they identify themselves.

Keep in mind that currently there are five living generations in America and four or five of them are employed in the American workplace:

- Mature/World War II generation (born before 1945) (combined)
- Baby Boom generation (born between 1945 and 1964)
- Generation X (born between 1965 and 1979)
- Generation Y/Millennials (born after 1980, but before 1996)
- Generation Z (born around 1996 until 2010)

One source refers to the last generation as Generation Z or Boomlets.[3] Eventually, given life expectancy and the desire or need to work longer, there could be six generations in the workplace.

Each generation is influenced by its own defining events and technologies. Everyone has something to offer a team effort.

There is talk in some quarters that Millennials are in charge and are running things. Not so fast. Millennials's contributions are substantial, but everyone's employment reality is in transition especially in the aftermath of a pandemic. Consequently, there is a need for collaboration, identifying common ground, and compromise.

In conclusion, by sharing your skills and knowledge, by operating throughout your career with integrity and dignity, by assuming responsibility for your career and respecting the rights of others, you will be on your way to soaring like a majestic, wing-spread eagle rather than working like a turkey.

---

[3] Tutorsllop.net, "Characteristics Generation Z." Blog, *Tutorsloop.net*, July 10, 2015, www.tutorsloop.net/characteristics-generation-zboomlets/

Your multifaceted and constantly changing working environment represents an unprecedented opportunity—an opportunity to learn and to soar. This is your time. Technology uniquely positions you to soar. Look forward. Reach out.

**R** also stands for **Remember:**

1. To make quality time for those who are important to you.
2. To be authentic.
3. Maya Angelou's quote: "Never make someone a priority when all you are to them is an option."
4. Only you can determine whether or not you are soaring. If you are happy and content, it does not matter.

## I Hope You Soar

Channel Dorothy Vaughan. Ms. Vaughn was a National Aeronautics and Space Administration (NASA) mathematician and computer programmer. Oscar-winner Octavia Spencer portrayed her in the Academy Award-nominated film *Hidden Figures*.

According to the film, Ms. Vaughn anticipated NASA's plan to replace her and her staff with computers. She proactively spent Saturdays in her public library teaching herself programming language. Subsequently, she taught her staff, and saved their jobs.

Ms. Vaughan and her staff were prepared for the introduction of machine computers and the programming language of Fortran. Self-trained, Ms. Vaughn became a computer programmer and ultimately led the programming section of the Analysis and Computation Division (ACD) Langley Research Center in Hampton, Virginia.

Ms. Vaughn's proactive approach to her impending employment dilemma is a model for personal career planning and strategy and staying abreast of industry changes. Consider adopting these strategies for your own career safeguards and advancements.

- Be a self-starter
- Do not wait for the ax to fall.
- Identify what you can do.
- Identify someone who can do what you cannot.

Do not accept rejection or defeat. Keep working toward your goals.

# Food for Thought

Below are edited excerpts from the transcript of Lou Alexander's interview on my podcast, *Your Employment Matters with Beverly Williams*. Lou is a former NFL athlete and Syracuse University graduate who has a degree in Communication and Rhetorical Studies. Please go to https://youremploymentmatters.com/blog/ to hear the entire interview.

### Beverly Williams

We were introduced virtually when you were the presenter at a Dulye Leadership Experience (DLE) virtual meeting hosted by a mutual friend, Linda Dulye. The DLE is an organization that develops rising leaders. Now please share your story, the story that you told at that virtual meeting.

### Lou Alexander

My name is Lou Alexander. I grew up in the inner city of Lynwood, California. Lynwood is a sister city of Compton, California. I'm one of 10 kids. I had to fight all my life because I've always wanted to be the best. As the littlest and the youngest, I always had to prove myself. My persistence and hard work came from my older brothers and sisters telling me that I needed to be the best.

I started to play football around the age of 15. I was overweight. Childhood obesity had a big impact on my life. When I transitioned to football, I found a sense of purpose. I had a sense that something was going to drive me to take health and wellness seriously.

I also believed football would keep me disciplined in the inner cities. I wanted to make sure that my mom wasn't worried at night about what her child was doing in the streets.

I was blessed and fortunate enough to be a really good athlete in high school. I transitioned over to prep school for a year. When I graduated high school after prep school, I received a full scholarship to play at Syracuse University where I met great people who were willing to help me.

After I left Syracuse, I was an undrafted free agent. This is where it really started to get interesting because I stepped into football, into the NFL.

I didn't know exactly what I was doing. I was a boy amongst men. The NFL was professionalism at its finest. NFL players had jobs. They had families.

As for me, I was a kid that was 22, 23 years old. I was in the NFL, but I didn't really take that seriously. I got cut and I left the NFL. I hit rock bottom. I didn't have any money to my name. I asked myself "What is next for me?" I didn't know what I was going to do.

I was about to board a flight to Boston. I had $22 in my pocket, $10 in my wallet, and $12 in my bank account. My mom bought me an airline ticket because I had a workout for the New England Patriots. I hoped to make the team, but something pivotal happened during that plane ride.

I got on the plane at LAX and sat in coach. I saw a gentleman wearing a nice suit and an expensive watch. And I'm like, wow, whatever he does, I'm quite interested.

This is where curiosity and courage really played a role, It took curiosity and courage for me to not only identify and look at that man (I didn't know him from a can of paint), but to say, wow, if I get opportunity to sit next to that guy, I'm going to ask him what he does. The only thing I have to lose is just him saying, "No." I have nothing else to lose.

When you're at the bottom, you sometimes need to dig deep. You try to find a way to let faith guide you.

When the guy sat next to me, I saw him open his laptop. I saw that he was doing a presentation. As I looked at his computer, I leaned over to him. At the time, I was 6'4", 340 pounds. I was sitting in the middle seat, so I was squishing him.

I asked him one simple question. I want listeners to hear this simple question because this simple question opened up so many other questions. I swallowed my pride, and asked him one question, "Can you help me?"

That one question "Can you help me?" was the moment that my life started to transition into what it is today. He replied, "How can I help you?" His reply to me and asking, "How can I help you?" gives me goosebumps because I remember how vulnerable I was at that time.

I just wanted the opportunity to have a longer conversation with him. I knew that my grit, determination, and all the things that I had would cause him to think, this guy is someone that I want in my life because he's willing to get it by any means necessary.

Two days later, I went to his office. We had a conversation for 45 minutes to one hour. It was authentic. It was pure. It was just a real conversation.

Ten days after that conversation, I was working for him as a sales rep in tech. And that's where I started my career. I never knew that that was going to be my career trajectory. Sitting here now I'm a director of sales at 30 years old. It took that one time on the plane for me to ask him, "Can you help me"? that literally transformed my life into what it is today.

## Beverly Williams

Don't sell yourself short. You thought about what to ask. You were focused, mentally prepared, and willing to work hard. If after making the connection, he hired you and you didn't perform at a high level, you wouldn't be where you are now. Don't sell yourself short.

## Lou Alexander

Absolutely, I did have an agenda. What I meant is I didn't know that I was going to have a conversation with a guy on a plane. No one could prepare for that again. We talk about fate. I just stepped out. But I think sometimes too, we do have to kind of premeditate things that we want to ask.

Luckily, I studied communication and rhetorical studies in college. I studied rhetoric and developed the ability to speak with emotion and to understand how to ask questions. I have to attribute a huge part of that to the professors at Syracuse University for really equipping me with some of those skills.

But what really made me curious Beverly and what really made me ask the questions and have that agenda is because growing up in the inner city, I've been asking questions all my life. My exposure has been limited so I had to ask questions about what else is it that's out there.

When I saw that guy on a plane, I put myself back in the inner city of Lynwood. I went back to that little kid that asked questions all his life about how to get to the next level. How do I get to the NFL? I put myself in the same position. I asked him questions like, "Can you please explain to me?" "What is it that you do?" "Okay, you work in technology, do you work on the business side of technology or do you work the backend stuff of the mechanics of technology?" "Are you the person that actually builds all the technological things?"

I was completely unaware of that world, and he knew that. I was genuine about my questions and open and receptive to what he was going to teach me. That is where we have to get as people. We have to understand that we need to ask questions and be receptive to the teachings of others. We shouldn't ask questions so we can say, you know what? I know what you're saying already. Why? Because you don't know what to say because we don't know everything.

### Beverly Williams

When I say, you know what you know but you don't know what you don't know and why you don't know, it sounds like doubletalk. But it isn't. The higher up you go in an organization, whether it's a corporation or a charitable organization or a sorority, or even a family, you know what you're told. You know what you hear. You don't know what you don't know. You don't know why you don't know because it's above your pay grade or position in the organization or family.

In the absence of having the information that allows you to make an informed decision, many times people assume. Generally, they tend to do things and make decisions based on limited information. That's why it's important to have a network, and a mentor.

### Lou Alexander

Many of my generation are all about instant gratification. Everything has to happen fast. I think sometimes we put ourselves in this box. We think that we're the best at everything. We're not.

When I first got into tech, I was terrible. I didn't know what I was doing in business. I didn't have the business acumen that I have now. I didn't understand the art of selling value over features and functionality. I didn't understand exactly what I was doing. I was just relying on my pure instinct, but that doesn't always do the job. I think what really helped me was when someone tapped me on my shoulder and said, "Hey, Lou, you're doing this completely wrong." I looked at him and said, show me why it's wrong.

Now I'm a director of sales and I manage 14 people. The reps that report to me may call me on something and say, "Hey, Lou, I disagree with that." I ask "Why?" They've got to validate why they disagree. If they explain why they disagree and it's actually something that is a better solution than mine, I'm going to validate that.

Before I did not know that it's okay to be vulnerable. I think vulnerability is the biggest thing for us. It's our Achilles heel that we sometimes just can't get over. I think we just need to learn how to be vulnerable and learn how to be coachable when we pursue whatever we're trying to pursue. The way I phrase it is to consider feedback even negative feedback a gift.

You need to be grateful. Even if you disagree, check to see whether there's some validity to what you've been told. Feedback, constructive feedback may be critical or negative. You know, people like to hear that you look for information, not affirmation, that you want to do better. You want to improve. You want to be the best you can be. And you won't be that if you keep getting, "Oh, you're wonderful. You're wonderful." Cause we aren't perfect.

It's probably hard to tell now listening to me, but I was a shy kid. As I said before, I suffered from childhood obesity. I was always shy because I thought I wasn't enough. Even stepping into college, I reverted back to some of those old ways.

The shy person that's coming into the workforce or coming into who they are as a person has to believe in their ability. I think a lot of times the people that are the most shy and quiet have the most information because they never talk. Their power is by not saying a word, when they open their mouth, people will listen.

I also ask you, who are you surrounding yourself with? Are you surrounding yourself with people that are shy as well? Are you surrounding yourself with people that are forcing you to come out of your comfort zone? Because that's what the pivotal moment was as well.

I wasn't great in business or in tech until I started to surround myself with people that were really great in tech, right? If I would've gone back to my neighborhood and surrounded myself with people that were in the neighborhood, I wouldn't have been as educated on technology or be a leader as I am today.

When you're shy, you've got to surround yourself with people that push you to be more than just shy. People who will help you.

You can express that you're uncomfortable with people when you address a question. You can say, "Hey, listen, I never addressed questions like this. I'm typically a shy person, but you know what? I'm stepping a little bit out on courage right now. I just want to ask little questions." Those simple words can be life changing for you because that's going to get you to the top.

You have to ask open-ended questions so you can get the person to talk more than you talk. If you're a shy person, ask the person a question. That's going to get them to talk about themselves more than you talk about yourself.

### Beverly Williams

I think you're right. There's no doubt. I remember hearing a story about Beyonce and her alter ego, Sasha Fierce. I tell young women to adopt a Sasha Fierce persona and practice it in front of a mirror. Practice being someone other than who you are.

It may sound schizophrenic, but I know from personal experience, as you move up in your chosen profession, whether it's plumber, whether it's airline pilot, whatever it is, you're going to find yourself feeling schizophrenic. You know how you talk to your family and friends is going to be different than how you talk to your boss and your boss's boss.

### Lou Alexander

I couldn't agree more. If you are on a journey, no matter what your profession is, if you are meeting with someone in person, I always tell my salespeople to write down the agenda and key topics they want to cover and practice in the mirror. Talk to your mirror and talk to yourself as though you are talking to a client. Like you said, it may sound a little schizophrenic, but I completely agree with you. That's a really great tip.

### Beverly Williams

Let's be clear. We adapt to our environment, situations, and other people. It doesn't mean that you're fake or phony. It means that you're flexible and adaptable. You adapt to whatever the environment requires.

If you are not adaptable, you are likely not going to be successful. That's just the truth.

Decide on who and what you want to be, what you want to have, and who you will surround yourself with. It's important. If there are people in your life who are "haters," who are negative about the things that you're trying to accomplish, beware! If they are family members don't kick them to the curb. As my grandmother used to say, "Feed them all with a long-handled spoon."

If you are on a path that will take you places, there will be people who are supportive and who care and love you. But there may also be people who try to pull you down no matter what the relationship. Don't stop loving them, but you save yourself.

**Lou Alexander**
You have to understand that you are going to be different when you step into another light. I'm just reverting back to myself because I know that I represent everyone else that's in the inner city. You're everyone else out there that's trying to pursue goals and be a professional.

I represent them and I want to speak to that. When you change and when you try to grow into something, different people are going to hate that. You have to understand that and remove yourself. When I went to the NFL, people hated that. I'll tell you this, that's all they thought I was going to be, was a football player.

When I stepped into this business and I went into pursuing business, they were like, "Wow," he can do this too. Again, I identified the people that were actually there for my longevity and for the betterment of me.

If you identify the people that are not there for the betterment of you, you have to remove yourself because I'll tell you this, they're going to pull you down and they're going to put more doubt in you than you put in yourself, right?

\*\*\*\*\*\*\*\*\*\*\*\*\*\*\*\*\*\*\*\*\*\*\*\*\*\*\*\*\*\*\*\*\*\*\*\*\*\*\*\*\*\*\*\*\*\*\*\*\*\*\*\*\*\*\*\*\*\*\*\*\*\*\*\*\*

Hopefully, Lou's story will inspire and motivate you. Success can be yours also if you seek information rather than affirmation. Move forward with the knowledge that you can achieve your goals, but it will take commitment and hard work. Failure is not an option.

# Toolkit

## Workplace Words and Phrases

1. "Hold your powder" or "Keep your powder dry" (as in gun powder) means Be quiet. Don't assert your position or take a different position from the group.
2. "That dog won't/don't hunt" means that is not a good idea.
3. "Think outside the box" means be more creative and less traditional.
4. "I don't have a nickel in that dime," "I don't have a dog in that fight," or "I don't have any skin in the game" means I don't have any interest or involvement in the situation.
5. "Chum in the water" means to incite competition among employees or a feeding frenzy.
6. "Drill down" means conduct a comprehensive, thorough review or have a thorough approach which includes details.
7. "Granular" means detailed.
8. "Get your hands dirty" means no matter how big or small the task, do whatever is necessary to get the job done.
9. "Is that the hill you want to die on?" means are you sure you want to take that position or make that argument?
10. An "elevator speech" is a 90-second, oral, self-promotional marketing pitch.

11. "Brand loyalty" means that you're not easily lured away from a particular product.

12. An "800-pound gorilla" is a person, usually an executive or a client, who generates a lot of revenue for the company or has a great deal of influence.

13. "Tough times don't last; tough people do" means hard, tough times will always come and go but, when tough-minded people hit a rough patch, they persevere and get through the tough times.

14. "It's better to have and not need than to need and not have" means be prepared.

15. "That's good feedback" means thanks for your input.

16. An "elephant in the room" is a subject or situation that people know about but, for some reason, are uncomfortable discussing.

17. A "stretch assignment" requires an employee to work outside his/her comfort zone by challenging current skills while acquiring new or additional skills.

18. "Soft skills" are social traits, such as personality, friendliness, helpfulness, and integrity.

19. To "micromanage" means to supervise with excessive control or attention to minute details. This management style has a negative connotation.

20. "Pink-collar jobs" are positions traditionally filled by women.

21. "360-degree feedback"[1] is an evaluation tool, which involves the acquisition of information about an employee's (usually a manager or supervisor) work performance from a variety of sources and stakeholders, including direct reports, peers, and customers, his/her direct supervisor, and a self-assessment by the employee.

## Marketing Pitch

### (Old-School and New-School) Networking

There is a heightened intensity that accompanies job searches because of the seismic shift in the employment landscape and the constantly

---

[1]  360 Degree Feedback: See the Good, the Bad and the Ugly, https://thebalance-careers.com/360-degree-feedback-information-1917537

changing terrain. Consequently, anyone who is looking for work should use all available resources aggressively and exhaustively because the great lead that results in a great job can come from anywhere.

**Objective:** It is to include all possible strategies and advantages in your job-search arsenal. You may be surprised by the number of people you know and how extensive your networks are when you list them.

**Preparation:** Maximize the likelihood of favorable job-search results by embracing both new-school and old-school networking. Both methods should be used simultaneously and vigorously.

New-school networking favors the speed of more impersonal electronic connections and submissions and social networks to share information and communicate thoughts, ideas, hopes, and dreams. Do not limit yourself.

Social media is a great tool. Unquestionably, tablets, laptops, smartphones, and various types of social media are useful devices and essential to achieving employment success; however, it is foolhardy to rely on them exclusively or even primarily

By all means, use LinkedIn, Instagram, Facebook, Twitter, texting, and any other form of social media and communication that connects you with people. After establishing an online relationship, tell them that you are looking for a job. Ask them if they can help.

Based on discussions as you establish the online relationship, consider whether there is anything you can do for the person you connect with on social media. Remember, as you network, it is helpful to create a "win–win" situation by doing something that benefits the other person.

Friends and other contacts may look you up on Facebook or LinkedIn or conduct a Google search before they refer you. Consequently, you want to make sure that you do not have anything on social media sites that hampers your efforts to find a job.

Old-school networking is person-to-person (and during a pandemic virtual) contact, especially referrals and recommendations. This approach can almost magically get a person in the door for at least an exploratory interview.

The reason: Given the number of talented, educated, skilled people looking for work, hiring decisions will be made based in part on intangibles, on first impressions based on personal appearance, and on the prospective employee's ability to communicate. Who knows whom, who referred whom, who is related to whom, who owes whom a favor, and who wants to make points with the person who made the referral may also be factors in hiring decisions.

Prepare a brief (no longer than 90-second) marketing pitch, which is:

- A self-serving, self-focused commercial; and
- An opportunity to highlight your attributes, such as verbal skills, poise, presence, and personality.
- The pitch should have the following key points:
  - Your experience, strengths, and accomplishments
  - The type of work or position you are seeking
  - Why you are interested in that type of work or industry
  - Why you are attending the event or what you are seeking (optional)

## Sample Content

If you are a recent college graduate and you are looking for your first job:

- Identify clubs in which you have participated and the contributions you have made (e.g., teams, hobbies, scouts, cheerleading, theater, soccer, tennis, sports, and leadership roles).
- If you are a member of a team or participate in sports, list the attributes (e.g., focus, practice, reliability, and teamwork) that contributed to successful results for the team.
- List experiences you have had that have contributed to your personal development (e.g., when you were a lifeguard, you were, among other things, reliable and trustworthy, and you paid attention to details).

If you have been out of the workforce for a while:

- Identify leadership roles (if any) and activities in which you have participated and the contributions you have made.
- Identify the skills that made you effective as a volunteer, parent, or caregiver.

*Sample Marketing Pitches*

- "Hello, I'm_____. It is nice to meet you. I just (graduated from/received a certificate or diploma from/completed training at) _____, where I (majored in/specialized in/focused on) _____."
- "As a member of the _____ (team/group/chorus/organization) in (college/high school/my community/my religious group), I contributed to the success of (identify the project/the effort/the event)."
- "As a volunteer at _____, I increased the number of clients we were able to serve by streamlining our enrollment process."
- "I'm proficient in Microsoft Office and other frequently used computer software programs. My computer skills have been described as impressive."
- "Anyone who knows me will tell you that I'm a reliable, hard worker, who is strategic as well as tactical." (Be prepared to provide examples that illustrate how you were strategic and tactical.)
- "I work well on a team, but I'm also a leader."
- "I get the job done! I deliver."
- "I go the extra mile to provide a quality product."
- "I can add value to your team or organization by working hard, being punctual, and paying addition to detail."
- "I'm willing to jump in to fill any void on the team."
- "I want to be your 'go-to' person."
- "My personal brand is best described in two words: hard worker."

# Personal Marketing Plan

## *How to Market Yourself*

Remember: Given the number of talented, educated, skilled people who are looking for work, hiring decisions will be made based in part on intangibles.

First impressions are critically important. You need a plan.

- Adopt a positive yet realistic state of mind.
- Conduct a self-assessment where you highlight strengths and improve weaknesses.
- Prepare and practice your marketing pitch.
- Research industries and businesses that interest you and to which you think you can contribute.
- Learn about the personal appearance required for those businesses and decide whether it fits you.
- Identify events where you will meet people.
  - Check various media outlets for possibilities.
  - Attend events at least once a week.
- Prepare:
  - Cover letters, résumés, thank you letters, business cards, and e-mails (with no typographical errors!)
  - Voicemail greetings
  - E-mail addresses
  - Introductions
- Learn the power of networking in the following ways:
  - Use the "Job Search Networking Log" on the next page.
  - Prepare a contact list of all the people you know.
  - Create a database.
  - Back up all job-search material on cloud storage and an external hard drive.
  - Attend or participate virtually in events and meetings where you can meet people who may be able to help you.
  - Thank all contacts who do anything to help you.
- Learn the power of social media in the following ways:
  - Evaluate your digital footprint.
  - Regularly check and recheck your social media presence.
  - If you cannot erase negative digital material, create a brief, honest talk track to explain.
- Use the "Before-You-Leave-for-the-Interview Checklist" to make sure that your appearance conveys the message you want to send at networking events or interviews.
- Practice, practice, practice.
- Take a break periodically.

# Career Plan

Goal: ................................................................................................

Target Date of Achievement: ...............................................................

Requirements: ..................................................................................

....................................................................................................

....................................................................................................

Research Needed: .............................................................................

....................................................................................................

....................................................................................................

Additional Education Needed: .............................................................

....................................................................................................

....................................................................................................

Additional Training Needed: ...............................................................

....................................................................................................

....................................................................................................

**Networking Activities:** ..................................................................

..........................................................................................

..........................................................................................

..........................................................................................

**Status after One Year:** ...............................................................

**Status after 18 Months:** ...........................................................

**Status after Two Years:** ............................................................

# Before-You-Leave-for-the-Interview Checklist

*This is a generic list. Adapt these suggestions to suit the industry and position you pursue. When in doubt, default to this generic list. It is better to be safe than sorry.*

- Personal hygiene
  - Bring a mirror.
  - Shower/bathe; use deodorant/antiperspirant.
  - Use perfume/aftershave sparingly or not at all.
  - Get a clean, neat hairstyle or haircut.
  - Freshen breath and clean teeth free of food particles.
  - Have clean, neat nails; avoid anything that draws attention to your nails and is a distraction.
  - Shave, if you are a man. If you choose to retain facial hair, trim it.
  - Remove leg/nose/knuckle hair, and any other unflattering visual body hair.
  - Use moisturizer or lotion for a healthy, well-groomed look.
  - Check nose for cleanliness and eyes for cleanliness and eliminate redness with eye drops.

- Clothing and makeup—females
  - Wear clean, pressed clothing that fits comfortably in either dark, neutral, or understated colors.
  - If you wear makeup, aim for a natural, effortless look.
  - Limit eye shadow and blush. Avoid vibrant lipstick shades.
  - If you wear jewelry, avoid large earrings, and limit the number of pieces of jewelry worn at the same time.
  - Your shoes (or boots, if inclement or very cold weather or snow) should be polished and in good shape. Make a trip to the shoe-repair shop, and avoid anything that draws attention to your shoes and is a distraction.
  - Pantyhose/stockings/tights should be clean, with no runs, patterns, or decorations.
- Clothing—males
  - Your suit or sports jacket should be clean, pressed, and fit correctly.
  - Select a white, blue, or pale yellow shirt with a tie.
  - Your slacks should be crisply ironed and in dark, neutral, or understated colors, worn at the waist with or without a belt, and fit comfortably. A belt should be worn if the slacks have belt loops.
  - Your shoes should be polished and in good shape. Make a trip to the shoe-repair shop, if necessary.
- Unless you are applying to be a barista, chef, or professional athlete, cover tattoos and camouflage or remove body piercings.
- Stand and sit erectly with your head up. Do not slouch or lean on your hand.

## Interview Preparation Checklist

- Research the company and person or persons who will interview you (if you know or can find out).
- Practice your responses to questions found on online interviewing websites. Be sure to include your skills and experience that match or are similar to those identified in the job requirements and qualifications provided in the job announcement.

- For telephone interviews:
    - Get up and get dressed at least two hours before the interview.
    - Drink a hot beverage to clear your throat.
    - Stand up during the interview. Your voice is stronger this way.
    - Do not do anything during the telephone interview that you would not do during an in-person interview.
- Several days before an in-person interview:
    - Research what is appropriate to wear to the interview:
    - Have a friend contact HR to ask what applicants should wear.
    - Ask someone you know who works there and who, because of his or her role with the business, has reliable information about the organization.
    - Try on what you plan to wear to the interview to make sure that it is clean and pressed, fits, and you feel comfortable wearing it.
    - Conduct a dry run to the interview location, ideally at the same time of day you will actually leave for the interview. You want to confirm that you know where to go, how to get there, where to park, and how much time it will take for you to arrive at the interview site with 30 minutes to spare.
- On the day of the interview, bring the following items:
    - Extra copies of your résumé, even if you have already e-mailed it to HR
    - Business cards
    - Work-related writing samples, artwork, and so on
    - List of references, including contact information
    - An umbrella, just in case it rains
    - Tissues
    - *Tide-to-Go* or *Shout* in individual packets because you may spill something on your outfit
    - Emergency money
    - Medication, if you take any

- As soon as you arrive for the interview, go to the restroom to inspect your appearance, and pull yourself together visually and psychologically.
- Remember to turn off your cell phone.
- Now, take a deep breath, relax, and be confident. If you have done the work, you are ready for your interview.

Go get that job!

Job search Networking Log

Date _____

| Name | Title | Contact Information | Referred By | Met at an Event | Date of Contact | Follow-up Dates |
|------|-------|---------------------|-------------|-----------------|-----------------|-----------------|
|  |  |  |  |  |  |  |
|  |  |  |  |  |  |  |
|  |  |  |  |  |  |  |
|  |  |  |  |  |  |  |
|  |  |  |  |  |  |  |
|  |  |  |  |  |  |  |
|  |  |  |  |  |  |  |
|  |  |  |  |  |  |  |
|  |  |  |  |  |  |  |
|  |  |  |  |  |  |  |
|  |  |  |  |  |  |  |
|  |  |  |  |  |  |  |
|  |  |  |  |  |  |  |
|  |  |  |  |  |  |  |
|  |  |  |  |  |  |  |
|  |  |  |  |  |  |  |

# About the Author

**Beverly A. Williams**, a former HR executive, multifaceted labor and employment attorney, arbitrator, and author, is a cross between Judge Judy, Whoopi Goldberg, and Jean Chatzky. As a result of her HR, legal, and literary experience, she has seen and heard it all. Beverly is connected to employment and career trends and developments and continuously listens to and advises Millennials, Gen Xers, Boomers, and others. She believes that we learn from and through each other, regardless of our differences.

# Index

## OTHER TITLES IN THE BUSINESS CAREER DEVELOPMENT COLLECTION

Vilma Barr, Consultant, Editor

- *The Trust Factor* by Russell von Frank
- *Creating A Business and Personal Legacy* by Mark J. Munoz
- *Innovative Selling* by Eden White
- *Present! Connect!* by Tom Guggino
- *Introduction to Business* by Patrice Flynn
- *Be Different!* by Stan Silverman
- *Strategic Bootstrapping* by Matthew W. Rutherford
- *Financing New Ventures* by Geoffrey Gregson

## Concise and Applied Business Books

The Collection listed above is one of 30 business subject collections that Business Expert Press has grown to make BEP a premiere publisher of print and digital books. Our concise and applied books are for...

- Professionals and Practitioners
- Faculty who adopt our books for courses
- Librarians who know that BEP's Digital Libraries are a unique way to offer students ebooks to download, not restricted with any digital rights management
- Executive Training Course Leaders
- Business Seminar Organizers

Business Expert Press books are for anyone who needs to dig deeper on business ideas, goals, and solutions to everyday problems. Whether one print book, one ebook, or buying a digital library of 110 ebooks, we remain the affordable and smart way to be business smart. For more information, please visit www.businessexpertpress.com, or contact sales@businessexpertpress.com.

CPSIA information can be obtained
at www.ICGtesting.com
Printed in the USA
BVHW041309030521
606350BV00012B/405

9 781953 349965